Dest

Sanity

The tumultuous, topsy-turvy tale about a
mother's love for her family as they navigate
through addiction, adoption, and death
(Based on real life stories)

Nancy Grieshop

cover photo: iStock.com/btrenkel

Printed in the United States of America
Published by Braughler Books LLC., Springboro, Ohio

First printing, 2018

ISBN: 978-0-9822187-3-0

Library of Congress Control Number: 2018960613

Ordering information: Special discounts are available on quantity purchases by bookstores, corporations, associations, and others. For details, contact the publisher at:

    sales@braughlerbooks.com
    or at 937-58-BOOKS

For questions or comments about this book, please write to:

    info@braughlerbooks.com

Braughler™
Books
braughlerbooks.com

Advance Praise

The author writes with transparent authenticity, it feels like a story being told over coffee, one friend to another. I many times found myself crying tears of heartbreak, but then laughing out loud before those tears could even dry. Such an amazing story telling of the ups and downs of unconditional motherly love as it relates to addiction. Bravo.

—*Kelli Davis.*

Cathartic. Joy. Pain. Love. Loss.

This is an emotional story of what drug addiction does to a typical unsuspecting family. I had to stop reading it at times because I do not read well through tears. And yet I couldn't wait to get back to it. My baby sister has written an amazing book. Some of it is downright poetic in the way she paints a picture with her words. Some of it is disturbing. All of it is riveting.

—*Jane Varney*

I've known Nancy nearly my whole life. In reading this book I now realize there's so much I didn't know; her hardship and agony come to life in this book. She gives an astonishing account of the horrors of drug addiction and how it disrupts the fiber of an entire family. She keeps the story flowing endlessly. It's written honestly and with no guile.

—*Ruth Anderson*

Nancy writes the way she talks. So, reading this book is like having a conversation with her. The story line flows seamlessly through the crazy events of a family dealing with addiction. It's an emotional roller coaster ride. This book is an enlightening easy read—hard to put down.

—*Jessica June Bair*

For years I've searched for a book about the social work experience—like what kinds of families we would encounter in the work place. This is it! It's written by a Social Worker about a family in distress; through their fears, and losses related to drug addiction. It's a good read and bound to be a best seller. I feel like I know the characters personally. I want to read more about them and look forward to her next book.

—*Kate Allison Hobbs*

This book will have you laughing, crying and hoping right along with Nancy. Nancy shares with us an honest and transparent view into the world of addiction and its impact on the family system. This book is a must read for families facing addiction and for those working in the addiction / mental health world.

—*Kristy Matheson*

Dedication

This book is dedicated to my children and grandchildren—especially my granddaughter who was made to leave our family too soon and under some very painfully terrifying circumstances. I hope to see her soon.

It is dedicated to addicts, alcoholics, and their families who are made to live under difficult situations which are out of their control in many ways.

It is also dedicated to people who choose social work as their vocation and profession. We carry out our work shielded in a cloak of ethics as sound as the vows of a priest.

Table of Contents

Introduction ix

Katie Part 1: Unsafe Harbor. 1

Chapter 1: My Early Life 3

Chapter 2: I Find the Love of My Life 23

Chapter 3: My Early Motherhood 29

Chapter 4: Rick's Teenage Years 37

Chapter 5: Rick's Early Adulthood 53

Chapter 6: My Own Personal Hell. 65

Chapter 7: Rick's Growing Family 71

Chapter 8: New Living Situations. 77

Chapter 9: Continuing Chaos. 83

Chapter 10: Getting Older, Finding Rick. 91

Chapter 11: Daisy Enters the Picture 107

Chapter 12: The Dominoes Fall. 113

Chapter 13: Now Comes the Funeral 121

Chapter 14: Gloom Despair and Agony on Me 131

Chapter 15: Our New Norm 141

Chapter 16: Six Months Later 143

Katie Part 2: Safe Harbor. 145

Rick's Eulogy. 147

Afterthoughts 153

Book Club/Study Guide Questions 157

Acknowledgments 161

About the Author 165

Introduction

We live in a time of horrifying, spiraling problems related to drug addiction. Drug abuse has been around since, well shortly after the mind-altering substances were discovered I suppose. So, it's nothing new. What seems to be new is the volume and variety of drugs that are so easily available, the number of people who become addicts, and the increasing number of people who die because they use too much drugs and/or alcohol.

In recent months Montgomery County, Ohio has been identified as the opiate abuse capitol of the country by NBC and other news outlets. That's quite a distinction. Watching the stories on local and cable news channels and realizing that this is right in my backyard is repulsive and nauseating. When I used to think of drug addicts, I'd picture someone who maybe started out in squalor, who nobody cared about, or was born into the world by a mom who got pregnant by some man who ditched her. Someone who possibly ended up in the gutter making money by prostitution and/ or selling drugs and they were probably in trouble with the law. But that's not necessarily the case. Conversely there are so many different scenarios, it's impossible to predict who might become an addict, just by looking at their family and social situation as a child.

These days drug manufactures and physicians seem to be at the helm of the epidemic. Drug companies convinced physicians that opiate derivatives used for pain were safe. Not at all addictive. So, physicians started writing out one prescription after another. A patient might see a doctor for a little cut or scrape and be given a narcotic. They would get another prescription when that was gone, and the cycle of addiction would be in full force long after there was a need for pain relief. At this point, Montgomery County, Ohio is on pace for 2018 to have an average of nearly three people a day die from a drug overdose. (Ohio Board of Workers' Compensation. Montgomery County: 521 accidental overdose deaths. 9/14/2018) A friend told me that eight people overdosed and died on just one Friday night in July this year.

Some confusing aspects of drug addiction are why some people become addicts, when others don't. Why one member of a family becomes quickly addicted, when his siblings don't seem interested in using drugs at all. Why one person can use Vicodin for a few weeks following a surgery and stop without giving it a second thought, while another can't live without it after just two doses. Why one teenager takes her first drink of alcohol, and drinks till she passes out—a pattern that continues every time she takes a drink while another person can have just a couple drinks most days into their eighties, and never seem to suffer physically, socially, or psychologically. Do genetics play a major role? Is it merely a matter of luck? Are prescription drugs and street drugs designed to make a person addicted by their ingredients, with stronger and stronger additives?

I don't know the answers to these questions. I assume there is some truth to the suppositions. I do know that statistics hit you differently when you're in the middle them and having an addict in the family tears it apart. Literally. It pits siblings against each other, children against parents, and sinks fear into the very fiber that had bound them all together. It often results in financial, medical, and legal problems. And there's typically resentment for the addict from everyone in the family. Then sometimes unfortunately, a child is left to be raised by strangers. Or worse yet someone in the family dies.

Using drugs excessively, never appealed to me. In fact, I was always scared to use something that came from a stranger or wasn't pre-packaged, inspected, and sealed. Sure, I sat with friends on the rooftop of the house I lived in while I was going to nursing school, and occasionally someone would bring out a joint. I never inhaled (So Bill Clinton, I know!). I do admit, I like beer. But nothing else. So, it continues to baffle me how my son winded up using a boat load of pot, and being addicted to alcohol, and cocaine (throw in some meth and heroin early on) while my other kids seemed unscathed by these problems.

Often in social situations, the subject of addiction will come up in conversations. I've had friends tell me recently that if someone wanted to get off drugs, they should just stop using them. Some folks will insist that if someone knows they are hurting themselves by their bad habits with drugs, it should be easy for them to quit. So somehow, they reason, once addicts are educated about how dangerous these street drugs are, they would, of course stop using them. Some people I know have stated that if someone overdoses three times, they should just be left to die if they overdose again. I wonder if they would feel the same way if it was their child or grandchild who overdosed. It burns me up to hear this kind of rancor when they are generally drinking alcohol and / or smoking cigarettes during their dissertation. So, they could be addicts too; they are just using drugs that are accepted in society and offer a slower dying process if used to excess. I'd like to see them just stop smoking and drinking cold turkey just because someone told them it was bad, and they had to quit. They have been educated about the dangers of using these substances, yet they keep using them. It makes them feel good to smoke and drink, what's the harm to anyone else? I'll bet addicts also think they are not hurting anyone else, and that it's no one else's business.

Another thing that baffles me is the attitude that some health care workers have toward alcoholics and drug addicts who go to the hospital when they get excruciatingly sick and go into withdrawal. Withdrawal, what an awful thing that is to witness. It must be hell to be the person experiencing it because it sure is hard to watch. I've been in the health care field for nearly forty-five years—as a nurse and then social worker. I see staff these days act disgusted with patients who suffer with addiction. I've seen a wife who didn't know her husband was in serious delirium tremors (DTs), even had a drinking problem. Then the nurses taking care of him say amongst themselves, "How can that be? How can a woman not know that her husband of twenty years is a drunk? If that was me, I'd dump his ass!" They occasionally make fun of these addicts and belittle them: "Why don't these people just stop (smoking, shooting up, drinking, and swallowing)? Police should stop giving Narcan, and let the suckers die. If they're not smart enough to stop using the crap, we should quit trying to save the jerks." What a compassionate profession we've become!

This book is a story about a family who has felt the pain of addiction and knows that it doesn't impact just the person who is addicted—it impacts generations of their families and friends. In some extended families, questions from outsiders about the addict are eventually no longer asked. Often the addict and his immediate family are shunned, and concern is no longer expressed. I've seen it become taboo to discuss it. For their parents, siblings, children, nieces, and nephews the pain, anger, and confusion never end. There might be a modicum of forgiveness for the addict, and possibly acceptance of the whole addiction process. There might even be joy and happiness as the person conquers the addictions. Yet the process of recovery and redemption leaves deep scars in the people who have loved them.

This is a book written about stories based on families with addicts. It's a story about the impact drug abuse has had on everyone in the family of an addict. It is based on my family. Being the mother of an addict is a heavy burden to bear. Watching a son sink deeper and deeper into the abyss as drugs overtake his life was pure torture. Not knowing where he is—if he is dead or alive for days, months, and even years—can become the norm. Getting back with an adult child once he overcomes the ugly cloak of drug abuse, can be a thing of real beauty. What strong, wonderful adults some abusers can become. The fact that some people have beaten their addiction gives me hope that others can do it, too.

KATIE PART 1

Unsafe Harbor

She was already subjected to the worst kinds of abuse. It started with exposure to different narcotic drugs and alcohol, malnutrition, yelling, violence, neglect, and sleep deprivation, among many other types of abuse before she was even born or had taken her first breath. She wasn't even yet born.

Her mom and dad didn't know better. Mom had used a variety of drugs since her early teenage years. It was her, and her family's way of life. In fact, she probably wouldn't know how to get through a week without them. She admitted to using drugs during her two previous pregnancies, and thought her older kids were okay. So why not with this one?

Her dad also got into drugs very young. But this was not his family's way of life. His family would drink socially—beer mostly. No hard liquor. No smoking, not even cigarettes. No street drugs or even prescription drugs. But drugs found her dad when he was in grade school and seemed hell bent to destroy him. Would the strong influence of his family, and upbringing be enough in the long run to save him?

How unfair to a baby! How could her parents put her in a situation that could potentially have a life-long detrimental impact on her? A situation that could result in emotional disturbances, learning disabilities, and a good chance of becoming an addict herself.

What was to become of this baby named Katie?

This baby girl who is my granddaughter.

CHAPTER 1
My Early Life

Sometimes I wonder how I got to where I am. How could I, a girl who grew up on a farm—having such a simple childhood, who wanted nothing more than to live out my life in the honored position of being the youngest in a family, hoping to get married to the man who would love me, stay with me till death do us part, and dance with me at our grandkids' weddings—end up as a grandma sitting home alone most nights. How did that happen? I gave birth to three kids. One of them started using drugs at a very young age. All of them married and started families of their own. Then my marriage fell apart. So here I sit rocking in Pop's old rocker, watching cable news. Alone. Except for my cat Tippsi—the most beautiful cat in the world. My grandson thinks she will never die. He just turned seventeen, and well, she's seventeen, too.

Maybe my life would have been easier if I had known someone who lived through challenges like mine. Maybe if I could have read something about how to navigate through those challenges I would have found better ways to deal with them. As it turns out, I still don't know anyone who has been handed the odd assortment of life events that I find myself continuing to deal with daily. Life started out so simple...

* * * * *

Of course, I was not spoiled as the baby of the family. Something eleven older brothers and sisters would probably dispute. I didn't really like being the youngest of the family when I was a kid. Now I love it. They're all old. My oldest sibling, Leo, is twenty-three years older than me. You got to feel bad for Mom. Twenty-five years of cloth diapers, and rags to clean up after us. Supper was on the table at 5:25 pm every day. One brother and two sisters Leo, Helen, and Mariam got married before I have any memory of them.

Leo would sometimes stop by at suppertime on his way home from work at the feed mill. He would catch up on our news and give us updates on his family. I recall seeing pain and sadness in his eyes many times. He had seven children, and his wife Dottie had cancer. After suffering for years, and being cared for in their home, Dottie died when their youngest child was two years old. I learned a lot about grief through her death. At first, I didn't understand it, and didn't know what to do about it. Mom and Pop were with Leo and his kids the evening of her death. I sat in the kitchen with some of my siblings; Hank, Mabel, Ginger, and Frances. I didn't know what to do. The kitchen felt dark and empty even in the light of a bright September evening, and the five of us sitting there. Frances was composed, almost stoic. She and Ginger had spent many days with Dottie through the summer. Trying to keep her comfortable. Taking care of her children as she got so weak she could do nothing for herself. Ginger tried to stifle her tears. Hank let her have it: "I don't know why you're crying. People die in Vietnam every day and you don't cry for them." Mabel who was quiet by nature and generally kept her opinions to herself, was acting as the mother that day, trying to soothe us, feed us supper. She erupted when Hank said that, and she actually shouted at him, "Don't talk to her like that! Dottie just died. She wasn't some stranger in Vietnam, she was our sister-in-law!" It got quiet. That set in motion for me the notion that in our family we don't get emotional, at least not sad, even in the face of death. How absurd, looking back. When can you get emotional if not when a family member dies? Leo married a widow with nine children several years later. The oldest in each set of kids was twelve. They had two more kids. Yep. You added right. Eighteen children in that home.

4

1: My Early Life

My sister Helen is someone I always admired, yet I wasn't always sure who she was to me. She took care of me when I was a baby then married and left the house when I was maybe two. I didn't really know who she was when I was in first grade. But I know her now. She is an amazing woman who endured her share of tragedies. Her husband Henry had a major stroke when he was forty-two. Their youngest, Mikey, was born with Down Syndrome. Henry died several years after a second stroke and Mikey died in his early thirties. Through all that Helen remains steadfast in her faith and involved in her church. She was always pretty much of a home body with all those kids to raise, but she went to Las Vegas with the rest of us siblings several years after Henry died. We took her to an Elvis impersonation show. The expression on her face when Elvis kissed her smack dab on her lips was hilarious and unforgettable. Later, she slowly touched her lips with her finger tips as she gazed off into the distance as if lost in a distant memory. I grinned in amusement.

Mariam is one of the more outgoing of all of us. She has a hardy laugh and speaks her mind. She had eight kids, all of whom are exceptionally successful in the business and medical fields. She also is a hard worker. Her acre-plus vegetable garden was the talk of the neighborhood. When I was in grade school, she had me come over to help get some of the ripe vegetables into the house to be canned. She was pregnant for the fourth or fifth time. She sent me out to pick the green beans. I was certain I was going to die the hundred-degree heat just ninety feet from her back door. I couldn't breathe. But I kept picking the beans. I was proud of myself as I braved the sweltering heat and picked every single bean off the vines. Eventually, I brought my bounty of beans into the house to show her. It filled half a bucket. She seemed a bit disheartened by what she saw as a scanty crop and later went out revisit the job I'd done. I'll be darn. She came back in the house with two over heaping buckets of beans. At first, I was amazed that so many beans could grow in such a short two-hour time span.

Now I realize I was bad bean picker. The experience made me want to do better in every job. She still has a wonderful garden. Just not as big. She's never asked me to come back and pick her beans. Waste of time I guess.

So, with those three siblings married and gone, I only remember there being eleven people eating together at the supper table. I don't remember when there were all fourteen of us. I sat next to Mom to my right. To my left was Frances, then Ginger. Around the corner from her was Alphonse, then Sparky Marky. Around the corner from him sitting on the bench were Patrick, Hank, and Vernon. On the end were Pop and Mabel. Then back to Mom. There wasn't much talking at the supper table, which seems odd now considering all the people there. Early on, German was spoken, and the topics were generally about farming. Sometimes there was a little gossip about neighbors, nearly all of whom were relatives. We little kids didn't talk at all because we didn't know anything. Or so we were told. Nearly everything we ate was home grown and homemade. Even turtle soup, if we were lucky enough to catch an unsuspecting turtle lumbering outside.

Pop was born in 1899. His parents were immigrants from Germany. Imagine the world changes he witnessed in his eighty-seven years of life! He travelled by horse and buggy as a youngster, and then saw a man walk on the moon when he was seventy. He completed sixth grade, then didn't go back to school because he figured he knew more than the teacher and maybe he did. He was very old school when it came to social and family issues. He believed his kids did not need college. The boys would farm; the girls would be able to leave home when they were married and had a man to take care of them. He was very out spoken, and I thought he knew absolutely everything. Pop was not one to argue with his kids. His word was final, and we didn't talk back. Ever. Especially if we knew he was wrong.

Mom was born in 1906. Her parents were also immigrants from Germany. As outspoken as Pop was, Mom was quiet. She

6

ran the house and he ran the farm. Pop would get involved with disciplining the girls only if we got out of line too much for Mom's satisfaction. That only happened a couple times for me. I saw what my older brothers and sisters got away with and what got them in trouble. I learned to keep a low profile and not get caught.

I have no idea about the disciplining of the boys now that I think back on it. I have a feeling that Pop's boot may have been placed at strategic locations on the boys' butts on some occasions. They kept quiet about it probably because they figured they would be in worse shape if they complained.

Pop bought a farm in between the one he lived on, and the one Mom grew up on. The land was mostly forest when they were kids and they spent a lot of time clearing the area, so they could farm it. They bought the one hundred twenty acres in 1929 right at the beginning of their marriage and the Great Depression. They had four children during the 1930s and even with the high price of dry goods and food staples, and the low sale price of farm products, they paid it off in ten years.

There was a certain amount of angst worldwide for people of German descent during World War II. This even applied to the folks living in our remote, farming area. The fear was that they would be incarcerated because of what Hitler was doing in Europe. They feared their kids would be taken away and put in cages, to die at some point. They had heard that the Japanese were placed in internment camps in our country and feared the same thing could happen to them. So, they blackened out the windows at night. They stopped speaking German in public. We still spoke German at home, and before I started first grade I understood and spoke German as well as English. Now I can understand very little German, but I can still scare the stuffing out of my kids and grandkids with some gruff words in German when I want to get their attention.

My next older sister, Frances, and I were very close when we were younger. She's two years older and sat to my left at the table.

I remember when we were pre-school age and the others all went to a one-room school. Yep, all my siblings went to Patterson Local the same school where Mom and Pop went. It was the last operational one-room school in Ohio and it closed in 1959, the year I would have started first grade. Vernon made the front page of Parade Magazine that year. He was carrying a bucket of coal into the school for the furnace.

Frances and I had long days playing together with the few toys we had. She had a doll, I had a teddy bear, and we had some Lincoln Logs that were of no interest to our brothers anymore. Believe it or not, that kept us busy day after day. We didn't watch TV during the day. When we could get it to work, we only got three stations on a black and white screen that was hazy most of the time. Pop liked to watch the weather on channel seven and then part of the Ruth Lyons Show to catch up on the local news. There were occasionally people from our area on the show. The TV went off when Pop went back outside to work. That was the extent of our daytime TV.

Frances came to visit Joe (my future husband) and me in Texas when we were there about a year. I introduced her to Vic, the very gifted, prolific man who became and remains her husband. I recently went to visit them, and I had more fun than I ever had with her in my entire life. Honestly, I never imagined seeing her play air guitar to Queen's "We Will Rock You" (May 1977 EMI label). She loves her Queen. Her time spent in the kitchen as a child has proven to be well spent, at least from my perspective. That girl can cook! Frances and Vic moved to Alaska after they got married. They love it there. It just goes to show that blood is thicker than water, and siblings are special. No matter how far away they live, or how seldom you get to see each other.

Ginger sat to the left of Frances. She's four years older than me. I always enjoyed it when I got to spend one to one time with her. Like once when she allowed me to work the hair straightener stuff into her naturally curly hair. I may have worked it in a bit too much one evening. She ended up with a bald spot on top of her head. That may have been the last time she let me do that. She also used empty lemonade cans after she washed her hair to get the amazingly straight, yet bouncy hair so popular in the sixties. She was more fashion conscious and sociable than me as I got into junior high school, so I paid attention to what she wore, and how she interacted with people. She was also smart and helped me appreciate the power of knowledge and travel as time went on.

Alphonse was in the Army and spent time in Germany when I was a toddler. He was nineteen years older than me and sat on the same corner of the table as Ginger. Whew boy howdy, he was mean to me when I was a kid. That was probably related to his drinking habits. Some of my earliest memories of him include him sitting in the recliner in the TV room, spitting blood into an empty coffee can. He fell asleep in that chair often. If I played a little too loud or maybe changed the TV channel, it would wake him up and he'd swat me good on my hind end. He eventually stopped drinking and turned out to be a nice guy. He died three years ago—the first of us to kick the bucket. I did the eulogy at his funeral Mass. I enjoy doing eulogies, as I tell the deceased person's stories. Even if the person had a crumby life, I like to find the humor and love they experienced. Even the priest laughed at some of my stories.

Next to Alphonse sat Sparky Marky thirteen years my senior. He was always quiet at home, but I saw him get kind of wild on the dance floor a few times. He was the first to graduate high school. He's not one to express emotion, but I believe he feels it very deeply. His quiet presence, sad eyes, and lack of verbal expression belie the emotions he experiences at, say, funerals. He's so quiet he didn't tell any of us he was engaged to be married when it happened. We heard it through the grapevine three or four days later. This would be the first family wedding in ten years. I was excited. I loved wedding receptions. The food, the dancing—especially square dancing—was fun. Marky seemed almost stoic about the engagement. Makes me laugh now at how quiet he was about it.

Patrick, ten years older than me, sat around the corner from Marky. He was much more outgoing, and even talked to me and teased me as a kid. I used to love going out to the milking parlor when it was his turn to milk the cows. We joked around, and it was fun. He had a very soft, loving spot in his heart. Once I saw him kiss a kitten on the nose and it grossed me out. About six years ago in October he was out farming, and somehow got run over by the tractor he was using as he slipped under it. He managed to crawl across the field over to his son's house for help. His recovery was agonizing, but he got full functioning back. The following June I took my friend, Tracie Jo, up to the Country Fest, in Maria Stein. Before the tractor square dances began, Tracie Jo bought Patrick a beer. He swallowed about half of it in two gulps, then he giggled and said, "The doctor told me last month I could have one beer a week. I'm up to Thanksgiving now." We all laughed.

Hank sat next to Patrick on the bench. He's more of a serious fella now. But he liked to have fun and push his boundaries when he was younger. One evening he let me drive a car home from the place he was to live when he got married. I think I was fourteen, he was twenty-two, and the car was a 1950 Oldsmobile. It was dark outside. I thought I maybe shouldn't drive it, but I wasn't about to turn down the opportunity. It was probably about a seven-mile trip. I was nervous and excited. The grass in the side ditches was about two feet tall. The country road was barely wide enough for two cars to pass. I knew the speed limit was fifty-five and figured that meant I had to go at least fifty-five miles an hour. There were no seat belts to contend with back then. It was suddenly decision time. A car was coming from up ahead and I was heading toward a concrete one lane bridge. Since in my mind I wasn't to go less than fifty-five, I decided to go over the limit and beat the on-coming car to the bridge and beyond. We all made it safe. With my heart nearly pounding out of my chest from the fear and excitement, I got home and stopped the car right in front of the kitchen window where Mom saw me get out. Hank got out of the car he was driving and laughed about how fast I drove. Mom asked if I drove the car home by myself. I didn't lie. She tore into Hank when she saw him. The only thing Hank said to me about it later that night was, "You should have parked in the barn yard, so Mom wouldn't have seen you." I felt kind of squeamish, realizing I could have died on that bridge. I couldn't wait to tell my friends at school.

Vernon sat on the edge of the bench. He's six years older than me and played with me more than all the rest of the brothers put together. We played basketball in the barn and wrestled on the front yard. Man, he could tease. He toughened me up a lot and still makes me laugh. After Hank and Patrick left the house, Vernon took over more of the farming with Pop. And I got to do a lot more work outside. I'd drive tractors to the fields during combining season, and when I was ten, I was allowed to follow the combine Pop drove round and around in the wheat field all day long. It was wonderful. Vernon eventually owned the farm outright, and still lives on our home place.

On that end of the table sat Pop then Mabel. I shared a bed with Mabel for eighteen years. She struggled in school and stayed up late at night studying her school books. She was the second in our family to graduate high school. She didn't date much in her twenties but had some fun girlfriends. Finally, she met a man she liked at the Crystal Ball dance hall in Frenchtown, Ohio and they were married when she was thirty.

That rounds up our supper table and my whole family. Sometimes unexpected things happened at that table. We didn't have an electric clothes dryer, so when it was too cold to hang laundry outside to dry, Mom would tie a long cord from corner to corner of the ceiling, criss-crossing over the top of the table. It was funny when a sock or Mom's bloomers would drop into the soup pan or someone's plate. God help us if it dropped on Pop's plate.

No one dare laugh out loud when Mom ranted about it and cleaned things up.

In general, the boys wore white T-shirts, and rolled cigarettes —Marlboro hard packs in their sleeves. When they smoked they frequently tapped the ash into the cuff of their blue jeans. All the boys at the time did that. They were groovy, man. The girls wore skirts everywhere and didn't smoke. It wasn't acceptable. We had to be respectful, wait on the men, and not interrupt. Blah, blah, blah.

⁎ ⁎ ⁎ ⁎ ⁎

Because I was the youngest in the family, every rite of passage I went through had been done by someone else before me— Baptism, First Communion, Confirmation, getting a driver's license, graduation, marriage, having kids. Plus, when I was two, I already had a nephew, with many more to follow for the next thirty-five years till there was a total of sixty offspring from my siblings and me. It was fun having kids to play with and boss around when my nephews and nieces came to visit. We had rotten pear fights and wrestled in the barn yard. Sometimes we would find an unhatched rotten banty egg. We discovered it to be very malodorous if we cracked it open. Occasionally we would find one with a partially developed chick inside. I marveled at the sight of a little peep that hadn't been given the chance to be born. It's tiny bones and comparative big eyes were amazing to behold. Then we would toss it haphazardly off to the side and let our dog Rover enjoy a snack.

Rover was the first farm dog I remember. Very obedient. Loved to chase things and bite the tires of visitors' cars as they ventured into to barn yard. My favorite child hood cat was Caffy Cat an orange tabby. No idea who named him. Caffy was run over by one of my cousins as he was disking out in the field next to our driveway; his leg was partially cut off in the process. I saw the whole thing. I also saw Pop take a hold of Caffy's front legs, step on the partially dissected hind leg till it was completely off. Rover ate the leg, a couple of crunchy chews and down the hatch it went. I cried myself to sleep that afternoon. Eventually Pop came in to talk to me. No hugs. He said the leg had to come off, or Caffy would die. This way Caffy would be able to make it heal. I accepted that and dried my tears.

Rover and Caffy were great mousers when we cleaned up the huge pile hog manure out behind the barn. Pop and Vernon loaded up the poop on the manure spreader. Then Vernon, Rover, Caffy, and I attacked the mice as they scurried from their shrinking mountainous manure mansion. Vernon stomped on them with his boots, till eventually he would be dancing and squealing when one ran up his leg. Underneath his jeans. I'd laugh and he'd yell at me to hit 'em with my stick. So, I'd casually whack them dead as they tried to get past me. Rover and Caffy would chunk 'em down whole as the mice tried to escape to safety. I shudder now remembering their swollen bellies which were filled with still living, moving mice looking for an escape route. They slept for hours after the job was done.

Growing up, I worked plenty hard on the farm. And I loved it all. Hoeing weeds in the garden and tomato fields, shoveling manure, butchering chickens and rabbits. Since I didn't like taking care of chickens or rabbits, I admit it was kind of neat on some sick level to watch the chickens flop around the barn yard after I took an ax to disconnect their heads from their bodies. I never knew chickens to show much emotion in a routine day, but their eyes were wide open in shocked disbelief when their heads were just lying there, while their legs ran a few steps with the rest of their body then flopped in a dead heap. I would knock rabbits out by hitting them with the side of my hand just behind their ears, then I would cut off their heads, skin, and disembowel them. I thought it was cool that their hearts were still beating when I cut them out. I couldn't eat rabbits when we had them for supper. It didn't seem right. None of that killing stuff would I be able to do today. It's appalling now to think that doing those things were a normal fact of life for me back then.

Cows were different. They had personality. Sort of. Anyway, I liked them. They were big, and I could put a halter on them and take them for walks—even ride some of my favorites. I hated to see them loaded up on the truck to be taken away and slaughtered if they didn't produce enough milk. I would seriously consider becoming a vegetarian when we'd be eating supper and I would figure out the main dish was a cow I had considered a pet. Yuck. Feeding the cows and milking them was time-consuming, hard labor. And getting kicked by a 1500-pound animal hurts bad. It happened to me more than once. It would bring a tear to my eye because it was so painful, but I don't think I ever complained about it. I just continued with the work at hand that needed to be done. And I tried to stay out of the way of the next fast-moving hoof.

The radio in the milking parlor and kitchen was always set to WOWO out of Fort Wayne, Indiana. They gave farm news, and local weather. I still remember the little song I heard so often in the morning, "There's a little red barn on a farm down in Indiana. Let me lay my back on a stack of new mown hay. In a barn yard where the farm land folks are pally, let me dilly dally all the live long day."

Once when I was in grade school, and was cleaning out the milkers, I got curious as to how it would feel to be milked. So, I stuck one of the milkers on my cheek for a little while and tugged on it a few times till I got tired of the experiment. Holy crap, did I get laughed at the next day in school. I had a dark red, perfectly round circle on my cheek. The teacher didn't say anything about it, but I think she stifled a chuckle now and then. I wonder what she thought.

I didn't exactly appreciate Mom calling me to get up before going to school so I could help Pop in the barn when my brothers had to do stuff in the National Guard—like go to the Vietnam War protests at The Ohio State University. For some reason, my next two older sisters, Frances and Ginger, never got the call to get up to help in the barn. That didn't really bother me. They wouldn't know what to do out there anyway. But still 5:30 AM comes early in the dead of winter, especially when your sisters got to sleep in and you need to go out in freezing weather. Mom would get me up by saying, "You can sleep later". Well "later" never came for me those days; once I was up, I was up. I can be thankful for that now—to this day I feel like sleep is optional if there's something else I want to do, like when I'm on vacation.

Of course, the other side of the coin is that Frances and Ginger had to do more cooking and cleaning than I did. Now, I did appreciate some good food and a clean house. I just didn't like doing the work to get there. I'd rather be outside. House work was something I found boring and uneventful, until I'd do something dumb like burning off my eyebrows when I tried to light the broiler in our gas stove under the oven. I had turned up the gas too high before I lit the match. Poof! The fire shot out about two feet and my face was right in the middle of the flame. Having singed eyebrows got a lot of laughs at school. I don't think anybody at home even noticed.

* * * * *

I have wonderful memories of spending seemingly endless days just being outside watching clouds float by. Memories of driving tractors. Oh, how I loved to drive tractors! We always had Allis Chalmers tractors. Memories of getting pestered and teased by all those people in the house. Okay, so truth be told I didn't really care for that—especially when I'd end up with a trip to the doctor for stitches or a broken bone...which did happen on a fairly regular basis: broken collar bone wrestling with my brother Vernon when I was five, clamps in my forehead from when my sister Frances hit me with a bat at age six when she was trying to figure out how to play golf and I stood too close to her, same collar bone broken when I was trying to learn how to ride a bike at age seven, BBB (badly bruised butt) when I fell off an empty fifty-five gallon oil drum that I was trying to roll around in the barn yard, three or four broken ribs when I ran into a tree playing kick ball at my favorite cousin's house at age eleven. That was especially memorable since, when I took off the rib brace, I had boobs. Boy was I mad about that. I didn't want boobs. They'd get in the way when I would want to do something. I didn't like the way they looked on me, so I put the brace back on quick to try to shove them back in. It didn't help. I still have them.

The list could go on and on. What impresses me now is that I never got any pain medication for any of these injuries. Even when I had an appendectomy—not so much as an aspirin or Tylenol after I got out of the hospital. I can't imagine kids going through some of that without getting prescription strength ibuprofen or Vicodin or even morphine these days. Maybe I would have become an addict by now if I hadn't learned to tough it out way back then.

It seems Frances and I had plenty of time to pester each other when the older ones went off to school. If we got too loud Mom would say, "*Yee fadolda clitzen! Hep yee keen fastant?*" Loosely translated from German, I think it meant "You bad little girls! Don't you have any sense?" I might not have understood it, but I knew that after she said it, and got out the yard sick, it was time to run. If we weren't fast enough, one or the other of us would get whacked on our hind end. And if we were too slow, we could expect to get an ear pulled. Ack, that hurt!

Mom was funny now that I look back at those times. She didn't like cats. At least not in the house. If a cat got in the house she would chase it around the different downstairs rooms with a broom. She would swat at it and yell, "Kitz, kitz, kitz!" I know she wanted the cat to go back outside but the door was never open while she swatted at it. I think I managed to not laugh out loud. But sometimes when a giggle slipped out I would see that look in her eye, and real quick cover my ears and run before she had a chance to pull them. I wonder if she would like my current cat, Tippsi.

Frances and I had measles at the same time, and chicken pox, and just pretty much did it all together. I really missed her when she started school, and I was home alone with Mom and Pop those two years before I started first grade. I spent a lot more time outside with Pop than in the house with Mom. I'd follow him around the farm for hours. He'd talk in German and I understood most every word he said. I'd be sucking my finger on my left hand and rubbing something soft—like the top of my cotton underpants—with my right hand as we walked about the farm buildings fixing stuff.

I knew instinctively how to have fun as a kid. Nothing' fancy just plain fun. But I still got yelled at a lot by various people older than me, and most of my brothers and sisters, probably related to the fun I was having with everybody around me. I don't know how it happened so often, but I frequently found myself in the middle of the action. Pop didn't complain over the fuss or loud noise that seemed to surround me wherever I went when we had company. He used to grin when I was getting into mischief and say, "*Do mus spas haben.*" Which also is German, and loosely translated means, "You gotta have fun." I didn't take that so much as an observation—more of a directive: "You must have fun!" I still smile thinking about him saying that. And I'm still trying to follow those orders! Oooh yeah! There's lots more fun to be had.

Pop also had an impact on my work ethic and life style. He liked to dance at weddings. He laughed when we had company. He interacted with every one of his grandchildren individually. But nothing got in the way of him getting his work done—completely, correctly, and on time. He continued to get up and work on the farm everyday into his eighties. This is grounded in one of my favorite bible verses from Ecclesiastes about there being a time for every purpose under the heavens (also from "*Turn! Turn! Turn!*" by The Byrds, released in December 1965 on Columbia Records).

And as far as lifestyle for Pop: church on Sunday, evening prayers (including the entire rosary prayed with the entire family), healthy eating, and minimal alcohol. His alcohol use consisted of up to two beers on the rare Sunday evenings one of my uncles came over with all their kids. He liked popcorn and homemade cracker jacks for evening snacks. I don't think he took an aspirin or any kind of food supplement till a few years before he died at age eighty-six. I remember once he got his arm stuck in some farm machinery. It was stuck for quite a while and it still surprises me he didn't lose that arm. He didn't even go to the doctor afterward. I never once heard him complain about it or see him take a pain pill for it. But thinking about the bruise on his upper arm still makes me queasy. It was nasty.

* * * * *

The thing I really enjoyed doing as a kid was playing softball. I taught myself, which is kind of weird because there were so many people around all the time. We didn't have good equipment. The gloves were probably made in the 1930s. One day I talked my older sister, Ginger, who is four years older than me, into playing pitch and catch with me in the barnyard. We didn't have a softball, so we used a croquet ball. You know, a solid wood ball. Well I was getting a pretty good throwing arm by then, and she was a light weight when it came to sports. I threw the ball harder and harder as I got warmed up. She missed a fast ball and it hit her square in the eye. She was a little upset to say the least. That was the worst black eye I ever saw. The white of her eye was completely red the next day. But it was hard to see her eye because her eyelid was so swollen there was just a tiny slit of space for her to peer through. I felt bad. I was afraid she'd bleed to death if she opened it wide. And then add to the trauma, she started ninth grade the next day. For some reason she never wanted to catch a ball that I threw to her again. From then on, she seemed to get even more enjoyment out of cooking and reading books.

Anything to not have to go outside and maybe have to dodge a croquet ball that I threw.

I missed Ginger a lot when she left for college—the old Good Samaritan Nursing School in Dayton. Then she got married to Jim who joined the Air Force, and away she went. I idolized them and their lifestyle at the time. It seemed so romantic and adventuresome. We remained close throughout our lives. I will always be grateful for all the help she gave me and our family as time went on. Jim died in a glider accident when he was thirty-five and a Major in the Air Force. That was traumatic. Ginger was left to raise her three boys alone.

❀ ❀ ❀ ❀ ❀

I had some good friends in high school, the good old Marion Local. Our group was dubbed "The Strohs Sisters." It was made up of Aggie, Sally, Lenore, Mary, Esther, and me. Apparently, we were considered the fun group in our class by the Strohs Sisters in the grade ahead of us. And we passed the name down to the fun group in the grade after us. I have no idea how long that elite club continued to be passed down, but it was an honor to get chosen for it. For just being ourselves. And well maybe because we liked to drink beer. Generally, on a Friday evening we would get a case of Strohs, go park somewhere and finish it off before we went bar hopping. We never got in trouble with the law and weren't promiscuous (for the most part!). We got good grades and were involved at school and church. Still today forty-five years later, my Strohs Sisters are my best friends. We still get together when we can and take trips together. I really appreciate this group of friends. We have helped each other through the difficult child rearing years, and our medical issues. We have clarified misconceptions of things that happened back in school. We continue to give each other serious reality checks as our lives move on in different areas of the country.

I grew up surrounded by people who were so homogenous—probably 99% of the people I knew through my high school years were white, of German descent, and Roman Catholic. The only family I knew before I left for nursing school who were Protestant, owned a junkyard. My pea-sized brain determined that all protestants were not to be trusted, were kind of messy, charged too much for their services, and would not be permitted into heaven. Of course, I got past all that. A few years ago, I heard a priest in an adult education class say that he when he gets to heaven, he fully expects to see protestants, and Muslims, and Jews, and Hindus right their beside him. He added that he feels the atheists will be really surprised to see God. Well stated.

I admit that I did date a Protestant from Versailles, a small town nine miles from where I grew up. That didn't go over too well with Mom. And it didn't last long. I'm certain Mom was embarrassed, ashamed, and figured I'd go straight to hell for even talking to him. Oh well, he was fun, and different. I ran into him a couple years ago at a farm auction. His family owned the food truck that served lunch to the treasure seekers. He was kind of sickly. He never did leave the area. Probably dead by now.

A deeply buried memory had me kind of messed up for several decades. I would become very anxious any time I thought that people might be laughing at me. It caused me different levels of anxiety over the years. There was a reoccurring dream-like state I'd find myself in. Something that would often fog over me when I got in situations where people were looking at me a little peculiar and I was uncomfortable about it. My mind would drift into an imaginary place that still seemed very real. In it, there was a little girl, in a very pretty dress, spinning around in circles in white patent leather shoes, and there was a bunch of adults standing around her in a circle, laughing. Like it was the funniest thing they ever saw. I felt bad for the little girl. Whomever she might be.

Finally, in my forties, my second oldest brother, Alphonse the one who used to whack my behind if I woke him up, asked me if I remembered when he got me drunk at our sister, Mariam's, wedding. I asked, "Did I have a pretty dress on? Were people standing around laughing at me while I was spinning in circles? Did I have on white patent leather shoes?"

He seemed surprised by the specific questions and said, "Yeah that's what happened." He got me drunk when I was four. Four! Finally, those haunting memories don't plague me. Now, I can laugh with people and not feel like they are laughing at me. What a wonderful thing to come to some resolution of that mystery. I can only imagine how long ago; partial memories of physical and drug abuse can haunt the living crap out of folks who just don't know what happened to them as a child. They might look at their circumstances in a different light, and not comprehend that something they can't remember is gnawing at them, keeping them from making rational decisions. As a result, they might not know how to change their lives for the better, or sometimes even manage to just feel good about themselves.

CHAPTER 2

I Find the Love of My Life

I met the man I intended to spend the rest of my life with when I was sixteen. Joe Wellkamp was a dream boat to. I met him at a political fund raiser at the high school in St. Mary's, Ohio. He and his parents made the chicken dinners. Some of my high school friends and we Strohs Sisters served the food.

The following Sunday Joe and I met at a CYO (Catholic Youth Organization) dance at the Carousel Ballroom near Celina. We joked for years about getting lost in "Baltimore" on the way home from that first dance. We took a lot of back roads and got the windows steamy. That was my first make-out session. And I liked it. I was mortified to see that I had four dark bruises on my neck the next morning. At first, I didn't know what they were, or how I got them. As it turns out they were hickeys—I didn't even know that was an actual thing back in my age of innocence. Mom thought I had impetigo and wanted to take me to the doctor. I was so embarrassed! Thankfully, she finally let it go. I kept my head bent over, and a scarf around my neck for about a week after that. Until there was no evidence of the supposed impetigo.

It seemed like Joe and I were made for each other right from the beginning—we certainly were an immediate hot topic. He was so sexy. And different. And fun. We would talk about religion, philosophy, spirituality, psychology, almost anything for hours on end. He was nothing like my brothers who were all farmers and liked to talk about which cows were going dry, which were in heat, and what would be the best day to haul manure. He was going to college and planned to get an engineering job. I wasn't at all sure what that all meant or what he would do with a degree.

At that time in my life a college education sure sounded better than sticking around the farm and wondering what was going on in the rest of the world. I wanted some adventure! Going to college sounded like it would fill the bill, for a starter. Plus, all the other Strohs Sisters were going to college. And the high school counselor told me I should go to college; I deserved to go to college. I can't believe I even had the nerve to talk to him about it. In my family, we didn't talk about family issues or our futures with administration folks at school. We did what Pop said we should do. Retrospectively, I'm so glad I took that step. It gave me the strength to apply to a nursing program at a community college. Sally, Mary and Esther were going there, too. I was thrilled to be able to stay with some of my Strohs Sisters for another year.

No one in my family had gone on to college. Ginger and Frances went to Catholic nursing schools. That was acceptable to Pop. A public run college—no way! There was no need for it at the time where I'm from, especially as a girl. Girls left home the night of their wedding. Pop told me I was not allowed to go because I would learn things there that I shouldn't know. He said it in German, so it carried even more weight since we talked in English all the time by then. I went anyway. He seemed proud of me when I became a nurse. I never did tell him I was going on to become a social worker. I don't think he would have liked it. He died before I graduated from Wright State University in 1989. He would never know that I got the Distinguished Social Worker of the Year award in 2011. I doubt he would have been impressed.

I don't think Mom ever understood the whole college thing either. She understood raising babies, cooking, cleaning, and praying. She got a letter from the Dean of Wright State, Celina branch when I went there. The letter was to notify her that I was on the Dean's List. I thought it was impressive. I felt like maybe I was not so dumb after all. But Mom seemed distressed when she showed it to me. All she said about it was, "What must we do to get you off that list?" I tried to explain that this was a good thing.

It meant I was getting good grades. It was more than she could comprehend. Oh well.

My boyfriend Joe had two older sisters and two younger sisters. No brothers. I couldn't imagine not having any brothers to pick on me and toughen me up. I also couldn't imagine not having any job responsibilities outside with livestock or farm work. He could go to the swimming pool during the summer or hang out with friends whenever he wanted. That was so different from my upbringing. He did have a paper route and got to keep the money he made from it. Conversely, I didn't get paid for my work on the farm. But I did get to eat, and sleep in a bed. His early life sounded like a dream childhood.

Joe's mom did get after him for a while to help in the kitchen. So, one day he had to dry the silverware and put it away after supper. He didn't just dry it, and put it back in the drawer, he bent the forks, then put them in the silverware drawer. His mom said he would never have to do dishes again, if that was the way he was going to do the job. I can't think of how I could have tried to get out of work by doing something like that on the farm. Maybe try to milk the hind teat of a bull? No, that wouldn't work. I'd be dead, or at least bruised up and broken. For years he and I referred to times when someone would get out of doing something by intentionally doing it wrong as imposing the "bent fork philosophy". And the people who did that kind of thing we called "bent-forkers".

A short time after we met, Joe changed his major and went into Psychology. That might have been some of my doing. I took a psychology class in high school and it really resonated with me. Well there are absolutely no jobs on a farm or in a small town for someone with a bachelor's degree in psychology. Cows, pigs, and chickens have no reason to change how they think or what they do. They just keep mooing, oinking, or clucking. His only other option was to work in a factory. That wasn't going to happen! It would be like throwing away his degree. So, we followed in Ginger and Jim's footsteps and Joe joined the Air Force. We were so in love. We didn't have two dimes to rub together, but our love would get us through everything. We just knew it.

So, I got married at a young age, twenty. I know, right? Coincidentally, our reception was at the Carousel Ballroom—the same place we officially met four years before. Our wedding day in February had the worst blizzard of that winter. In fact, the scaffolding blew over on my uncle's car. And Joe and I were left stranded in the parking lot when our car wouldn't start. We tried to wave people down for help. They waved and smiled good-bye as they drove off. Maybe that was foreshadowing. We'll see.

Joe left for boot camp in the Air Force at San Antonio, Texas in March 1974 three weeks after we were married. I left home to join him six weeks after that. I got up at 8:00 that morning in April. I went to get a U-Haul carrier attached to the roof of my Pontiac Ventura and I loaded up all our belongings inside. I grabbed our cat, Black Kitty, and drove to Dayton to drop her off with my sister Frances. I was so keyed up by the time I got there, and so anxious to start my new life with the man I would love to the ends of the earth, that I took off for my new destination at midnight that same day.

The atlas I used for travelling was as big as a normal-sized personal check-book. There were staples in the middle of the booklet right through Minnesota and Texas on the map. The distance didn't look all that far on the map. But driving fifteen hundred miles alone is far. Plus, the speed limit had been lowered to fifty-five everywhere in the US earlier that year, so my gas pedal foot would have to take it easier than usual. Plus, no cruise control. Which meant variable speeds the whole way. Also, the car was equipped with AM and FM radio only, so the music would come and go as I travelled. When I was driving in Kentucky on my way to Arkansas, I realized that for every four hours of driving, I moved less than a half inch on my map. Maybe I should have thought through this trip a little more. It was too late for that;

I was on my way. I got to Waco, Texas at midnight after being on the road for twenty-four hours. I got a hotel room. I was exhausted and excited. I took a shower and put curlers in my hair and flopped into bed. I wanted to look good for Joe the next day.

There were no cell phones back then. Our plans were for me to meet Joe at the Non-Commissioned Officers (NCO) Club somewhere on Lackland Air Force Base in the afternoon whenever I got there. He would wait close by the pay phone that I would call. Hopefully if I called, nobody would be on that phone and he could answer. I had no other way to contact Joe if something happened and he couldn't contact me if his plans changed. That was another thing we maybe should have thought through a little more.

The morning finally arrived. I was on the road again by seven. Just one hundred eighty more miles and we would be together. I don't even know what happened that day, but I didn't connect with Joe till six that evening. I found the Air Force base and was allowed it with no problem. But finding the place where Joe was waiting for me took hours. As it turns out, I drove around in ever changing circles until I decided to go into a place that didn't look too scary. And there he sat at the bar of the place I was looking for. Air Force uniform. Air Force haircut. Air Force issue black plastic glasses. What a sight to behold. We sat for a while and got caught up on things. Then went to our base housing for the night.

The next day we set out to get an apartment and moved in. All the stuff in my car took up basically no room in our tiny one-bedroom apartment. Somehow in the next few weeks, we got empty wooden electric wire spools to use for tables. And tied stacks of newspapers together for kitchen chairs. We slept in sleeping bags on the floor. It's just what we did. Even with nothing we felt on top of the world. We were together, living an adventure.

The days were long, hot and more humid than I had ever experienced. The air was so thick it seemed like you needed a knife to cut it, so you could walk through it. We couldn't afford to do much besides just breathe. So, we played a lot of tennis and cards. The card games were euchre and rummy mostly. We did go to beer calls on Fridays after Joe got off work. Through them I finally started getting to know people. Eventually I got my nursing license transferred to Texas and got a job in a doctor's office. After a few months we felt like we were standing tall and figured we had the worst behind us.

We had lots of interaction with fellow military personnel. It's true that the military becomes your family. Unless a spouse works off the base, it's hard to meet other folks. I found out what a hairy buffalo party was—everybody brings a bottle of alcohol which is poured into a trash can. Just add fruit, and a bottle of Everclear alcohol. And voila! Hairy buffalo! That's exactly what you felt like the next day. A hairy buffalo that the Indians had run off a steep mountainous cliff to kill them. It took a while for some partiers to recover from them. We also learned to love country music, especially Texas country music. We saw Willie Nelson live four times. We went to chili cookoffs, and area festivals. It got to be so fun.

Then I got pregnant three years after we moved there. And the nature of my life changed. My eldest was born in San Antonio nearly forty years ago. Within four years he had a little brother, and sister. What a forty years it's been...

CHAPTER 3

My Early Motherhood

I remember thinking, while I was pregnant that first time, that I probably just had a green blob growing in my belly. I didn't feel like I was a good enough person to give birth to a real human being. So bad had my sense of self-worth become in the years after high school. Thinking back on it, I'm not sure why I no longer felt good about myself. Maybe the adjustment of being so far away from home, not knowing anyone, and not having any money had something to do with it.

Anyway, after a long (fourteen hour), terrible, painful labor, I didn't even want to look at the little one. Finally, I did look at him, and hold him. I didn't give birth to a green blob at all. He was a real live baby with a huge bruise on his head. All the pushing left him with a great big, black and blue head. I also learned in that process that episiotomies are a pain in the butt. For real. We named him Richard—it means strong, powerful, brave—and wondered if he would live up to it. Of course, he would, we agreed.

What an adjustment it was to be a mother. Especially with a baby who absolutely would not sleep at night during his first year. Or second year for that matter. Plus, since I had to stop working to take care of my little rascal, so we had no money. Again. Also, we only had one car. For Christmas I made myself a top, Rick got one toy, Joe got a shirt and we splurged and got a blender, so I could make baby food and not have to buy it bottled.

Once he started sleeping better, Rick turned into a wonderful little kid—so loving, affectionate, inquisitive so happy. There were horses in the field out behind our house in southeastern San

Antonio. One day when he was still in diapers, I glanced outside and there he was—walking underneath one of them. Yikes! He seemed to be talking to them in a language only they understood. Like he was a horse whisperer. He had no fear of them. I cautiously went out to get him. Once I picked him up all hell broke loose. I thought he was just mad that I took him away from his "friends." But no. Much worse. He had fire ants in his diaper, and they were biting holes in his little butt. I think I lost the ability to detect high tones that day. That kid could scream!

Josh was born two years after Rick. He just popped right out after two hours in labor. Rick loved him from the instant he saw his little brother. He wanted to spend every second with Josh. And Josh looked to his big brother for companionship and learning experiences. It was fantastic having two little boys in the house. They played very well together. They didn't care where they lived—they just were happy wherever they were. As long as they had each other they were happy. Adjusting to having a second child was easy compared to having the first one. I just packed them up and took them with me.

After living in Texas for six years, I wanted so badly to move back to Ohio. I wanted my kids to know their grandparents and get to play with their cousins. Family is everything to me. So, when Rick was three and Josh was one, we moved to the Dayton area.

Dayton was kind of scary to me when I was a kid. Back then, if I would go shopping with people in my family at the Salem Mall, I noticed they would clutch their purses close to them if they saw someone who looked quite a bit different from them, like if they had dark colored skin. Just driving through north Dayton, terrified some of my folks. They would lock their car doors and roll up their windows—even in ninety-degree heat and with no air conditioning. I'm not sure what they thought would happen. But they seemed scared. Really scared.

Truth be told, when we moved back to Ohio, I wanted to be closer to my family than Dayton, which is fifty miles away from where I grew up. I was glad to be back in Ohio, although I really wanted to be closer to the farm. During my late teenage years, I couldn't wait to leave the place where I grew up. But having kids of my own, changed all that. After we moved, I spent as much time as I could back on the farm. Sometimes I even got to drive the tractors—they still had the same Allis Chalmers 45 as they had when I was a kid. I visited each of my brothers and sisters the first several years we were back in the area, dragging Joe and the kids with me. We got to as many family events as we could.

I felt safer in Ohio. There were so many unknowns for me in San Antonio. I felt like couldn't trust strangers there when I was out in public with my kids. I wasn't aware of any drug problems there, but just living in a town of a million people and I wasn't related to any of them, was not where I wanted to raise my kids. Looking back now, it's weird to realize that I was in the minority there in the workplace. There were more Mexican Americans than "gringos" like me. There were even more African Americans than "honkies", or "pecker woods" like me. In a work situation I had to prove myself to each one of them to gain their respect and be trusted. Once I was called into the charge nurse's office. She didn't come right out and say it, but she didn't like that I was fraternizing with the blacks and Mexicans. I thought I was just socializing the way I did with everybody else in my life. It was reverse discrimination from the way things were at home. I'm so glad I had that experience. It makes me more empathetic to those who are different from me and have to deal with white people.

When their little sister, Sophie, came along, Rick was nearly four and Josh was two. The boys included her in their adventures as well. I will have to say that she got the short end of the deal lots of times. She probably wished they'd just ignore her the biggest part of every day. They could be mean, without seeming to give it a thought. She would often sit behind the couch and draw on paper for hours all by herself, I think just to be away from their line of vision and attention. She dearly wanted them to leave her alone.

She was so quiet that we would often be in the car ready to go somewhere, and realize she was still in the house. Behind the couch, drawing.

Sophie did learn early on how to stand up for herself. For instance, one Saturday evening we were all at the Legion picnic in Maria Stein, Ohio when she was about four, and she was trying to get my attention. That's a hard thing for a quiet, little four-year-old girl to do when I was involved with some rare adult conversation. I heard her say with increasing volume every time I ignored her, "Mommy." "Mom." "Mommy." "Mother." "Mrs. Wellkamp!" Finally, she very loudly, clearly called out, "Nancy!" That got it. I immediately responded. She had to go to the bathroom. Like, right now. She's called me Nancy ever since.

During the two years of having three preschoolers, I began feeling isolated in my own home, in a town of thirty-five thousand people. Plus, we had no money, so I couldn't really get out and about. Joe travelled for a week or two at a time, so it was impractical for me to get a job. That was back in the day when interest rates were astronomical. Like thirteen percent for our mortgage which was $600 a month for a $37,000 house. Joe took home just over $1200 a month. We had to come up with a car payment, pay utilities, and buy food out of the rest of the money. It was tough. One day I was hanging clothes out on the line in the backyard, and I heard a car go by. I thought, "Dang there's life out there!" That eventually inspired me to go back to college. I wanted to be part of what was going on outside of my yard. I wanted to be involved and have friends. I missed the comradery of the Strohs Sisters and started renewing a close relationship with them.

I tried to raise my kids in much the same way that I was raised. I restricted the amount of time they could watch TV. We played outside together a lot. I wanted them each to know how to cook, clean and do laundry, as well as fix a car and take care of a yard. What I wasn't accustomed to because of growing up on a farm, and then living in town was having other kids so close by.

They could go to neighbors' homes every afternoon, not just on Sundays from two to four o'clock in the afternoon like we could do. Soon enough, personal computers, and hand-held electronic game machines were common, and the kids seemed to prefer them to me.

One of my favorite memories of Rick and Josh was when Rick was in second grade and seeing the two of them walking hand in hand in the backyard after school. I'm sure they were talking about the adventures of their day. It was so endearing to watch them. They really loved each other.

Of course, not all adventures turned out well. One day I heard some screaming abruptly coming from the basement where the boys had been playing. Rick calmly sauntered upstairs without a care in the world, and said the couch fell on Josh's head. Oh geez. I'm still not sure how it happened but after Josh got his head unstuck from under the couch, I saw he had a tooth that was shoved clear up in the middle of his face. It was so high it didn't even show through his gum. I lost a few more decibels of sound that day. Josh could squeal, too!

Lots more happened in that basement that I didn't hear about till many years later. It's probably best I didn't know at the time. My grip on sanity might have started to ease away even sooner. Eventually I figured out, there were many hiding places for Rick's drug stashes. I was told he even grew mushrooms down there. Not the kind I would cook, but the kind that makes you feel weird and hallucinate.

Of course, I admit that I was able pull some things over on them, too. Like the time Rick was standing in the bathroom, peeing in the toilet. It was early evening. I could see him. I don't think he could see me. There was an open window in the bathroom and I could see his head from the backyard. I snuck over and yelled, "Boo!" He screamed and pooped while he was standing there. He looked on the floor behind him, and yelled out, "Mom!" like I had done something wrong. I was laughing so hard, I could barely tell him I'd clean it up. That was when I realized I really could scare the crap out of someone. He seemed to still love me even after that stunt.

I always had supper on the table when Joe got home from work. I thought it was important for me to do that. I thought that's what Mom would do. One day I had slaved in the kitchen for hours. I made fried chicken, mashed potatoes, gravy, and green beans. It took all of seven and a half minutes for them to inhale the food, then they all ran outside to play. I started cleaning up the kitchen feeling indignant about doing all the cooking and then having to clean up the mess all by myself. Joe came back in the house and stood there looking at me. My thought was—oh good he's come to his senses and is going to help me with the cleanup.

Instead he leaned against the doorway between the breeze way and kitchen and said, "I want to know what's wrong with you. This is a perfectly good time for you to play with us in the backyard, and you'd rather be in the kitchen doing the dishes!"

I was flabbergasted. Didn't he know the dishes were supposed to be washed immediately after supper? Then they had to be wiped off with a towel and put away before any bubbles dried on them. That was Mom's rule when I was a kid. I figured it should be our rule, too. Besides I had played with the kids all day. I was ready to have someone do something for me. Then I thought back to the bent fork incident from when Joe was a kid, and decided my kids were not going to be bent-forkers. The next day we started on a schedule. Each of the kids—ages eight, six, and four had a job to do after supper going forward. One would clear the table, another would wash the dishes, and the other would dry the dishes and put them away. Before any bubbles could dry on them. That schedule continued till they got jobs outside the house. As it turned out, I think everybody appreciated it. Even Joe. He got to spend one-to-one time with the kids as he put the forks in the drawer. Without bending them.

There were occasional times as early as his grade school years that I was puzzled about some of Rick's behaviors. Some mornings I would get him up for school, and he looked like he hadn't slept all night—yet he was dressed in clean clothes, ready for school. I found this puzzling, but nothing to be concerned about. Or so I thought.

CHAPTER 4

Rick's Teenage Years

In no time at all, innocent childhood turned into the confusion and disruption of junior high school and the teenage years. It seemed like the vice principal took a notion to call me at least once a week to address this or that related to something Rick had done. Mostly the things were just stupid pranks. Like taking a laser light to school. He would sit in the back row of the classroom and point the red light on the teacher's head as the teacher wrote on the blackboard. Keep in mind that this was in the day when laser lights were brand new. Most people had never seen one—or even heard of them. I know I hadn't heard of them until the vice-principal called to tell me about the incident. Rick was such a cutting-edge guy when it came to stuff like that. By the end of winter quarter, he was either in detention for doing something dumb, or suspended for doing something really dumb nearly every week. I tried to talk the vice-principal into just combining the times Rick wasn't allowed to be in school with the times he had to stay longer—you know, wipe the slate clean. Just let him go to school during regular times and skip the extra weekend and after school stuff. But the vice-principal didn't go for it. The detentions and suspensions continued.

Now, I can't say that everything about Rick was all bad. In fact, he was a real sweetheart at times. He insisted on sitting on my lap in the big chair in the living room with me way into his fifth grade of school. For Mother's Day one year, he insisted that I stay home and be sure to answer the door if someone came over. Sure enough, the doorbell rang and four members of the acapella choir from the high school were on the front porch. They were dressed in tuxedos and formals. They sang *"The Rose"* (McBroom, 1979), one of my very favorite songs. Oh my God, it was beautiful. I got teary eyed as I stood and smiled and listened.

His behavior and getting into trouble had a detrimental impact on Josh and Sophie. Rick consumed so much of my time, just taking him to school and back home for the detentions and in-school suspensions was a lot. And never mind all the discussions—trying to understand why he was doing what he was doing. And mostly, telling him to just stop it. I really can't imagine how awful this must have been for Josh and Sophie. They knew more about what he was doing than I did, and they probably wondered why he got by with so much bad stuff. Stuff they would never consider doing. His actions impacted his siblings in ways I still cannot wrap my head around. It's hard to forgive myself for what was happening and how it impacted all of us as a family.

But Sophie helped me a lot. She and I talked regularly during these years about the insanity that surrounded Rick. He brought the insanity into our family. It impacted the very nature of our family unit. It strained every conversation with him. It just didn't make sense. Why couldn't he be normal, like the rest of us? I'll never forget Sophie saying, "You can no more make him be more like me than you can make me be more like him. He is who he is. And I am who I am." I agreed with her and from then on, I always considered her to be wiser than I'll ever be. I also tried to accept what he did. That wasn't always easy. Or even practical.

Josh was a bit more disengaged from the whole Rick mess and he didn't seem to want to talk to me about my fears, or his, concerning his brother. Everything else in Josh and Sophie's lives was going great. They were doing everything right...decent grades, no trouble with the law, good friends, and fun to be with. Josh played basketball, softball, and pee-wee football. He was planning to be the next Bo Jackson. He said he would be a pro in basketball, baseball, and football and do Bo one better. I threw a lot of softballs, baseballs, and footballs to Josh in our backyard. He promised me a big house with a pool for helping him be so good in sports, once he made it big. I'm still waiting.

Sophie played soccer, volleyball, and softball. I threw lots of softballs to her too. Sometimes Joe would come out and tell me to not throw the ball so fast to her. She was a girl after all. But she never missed. And I didn't use a croquet ball so if she would happen to miss, it wouldn't hurt all that bad. I'd tell her to hold her glove out about a foot from her left shoulder, and I'd throw the ball right in it. Fast. Just ask her. She'll tell you. She's never been afraid of a ball coming at her. She never had a black eye. It was good training for her for when she played softball in high school, and even after.

I continued to try "fix" Rick. I don't think I can ever make it up to Josh and Sophie.

◦　◦　◦　◦　◦

My cousins, John and Julie, had a profound impact on Rick. They had six acres of mostly wooded land outside of Bellbrook, Ohio and were clearing some of it to put up a log home. Rick worked for them many weekends for several years as they put up their beautiful log home out in the woods. Rick learned how to cut down trees, operate big power equipment, and how to be a master builder from them. All these things would prove to be things he needed to be able to do in years to come. He was good at all of them because John took the time to teach him right. They were like a second set of parents for Rick. John had the patience of a saint when it came to getting the job done the way he wanted it. John told me once that he noticed Rick would watch him do something, and then ask him why he didn't do something in a different way. John would listen to Rick's suggestion, and often Rick had a better way of doing the job. Julie saw to it that Rick was fed and safe while he worked for them. One day, Rick had a head-ache, so Julie gave him a couple aspirin. He took them without water. Julie went ballistic, telling him he would bleed to death if he didn't eat or drink something with that aspirin. Nothing bad happened. Rick and I giggled about that for years to come.

* * * * *

And then, here come the high school years. OMG, how incredibly...unpredictable!

Softball was a major source of interaction, socialization, and just plain fun starting from when Rick played T-ball in kindergarten. Once he started playing in high school, wow! Joe and I each coached in these recreational teams. In fact, I coached for seventeen years. I loved watching Rick play softball. He was such a natural athlete. So lithe. So fast. He had such good ball sense. Never felt a need to practice. And he was so fun to be around out there. During his senior year he got an entire traveling team together in just a few hours. That year, our three kids were on a total of five teams, and I coached three of them. I was out there at the ball fields six days a week, and I loved it. I was good at it. I finally felt like I belonged there. It reminded me of my youth when I played softball. All those years of living near Dayton and wishing I could be closer to my extended family, it was softball that finally made me feel at home and good about myself again.

Rick's school presence in high school was not so grand. He continued to get into trouble. I never knew what to expect. One day I got a call from the principal. Rick was suspended for putting a sign on the back of a student. Even worse, the student was one of the few African Americans in the entire school. I figured, very innocently, that the sign probably had something like "Kotex" or "poop" written on it. That's the kind of stuff the boys in my class would do, back in the day.

When he got off the bus after school that day I lit into him. How could he do something like that—and on the back of a black student? I was way into teaching him respect for all people, but it didn't seem to be working. In fact, he had a bit of a smirk on his face more like a shit eating grin. Finally, once I realized I wasn't getting anywhere, I asked him what the sign said. "I support gay rights" was his response.

At that time, the subject of homosexuality was taboo. Nobody talked about it. Not in public. Not in private. Not in the news. I was speechless when I learned what the sign had written on it. I sent him to his room. For a few days, I feared some type of retaliation from the black student and his family. I just knew that someone was going to come over and beat Rick up for putting a sign like that on his back. And then they would beat me up for being his mom. That weekend, Rick, the black dude and some of their friends played basketball at the park near our house. They worked things out. No hard feelings. I don't know what happened to the fella, but I admire him still. I can't imagine what it was like for him to grow up in a place where he probably had a really hard time fitting in just because of the color of his skin. And more than likely felt hated because of it. Then to have my son harass him, and finally to reach back out to Rick and make things right. That takes balls!

Rick didn't seem to be able to keep his driver's license very long during his last two years of high school. So, he spent a lot of time riding his bike. His bike was not all that great. It was a modification of a Stingray BMX bike. And old, with a lot of miles and hard riding on it. One late evening in early spring he called home. He merely said, "Mom."

I was a bit confused, and said, "I thought you were upstairs in bed!"

He wanted me to pick him up claimed he'd ridden his bike to Hara Arena, then got lost on his way home and ended up at Rolandia Golf Course. Now it was dark, and he felt he shouldn't ride the bike home. Crap. He expected me to believe that? That was thirty-five miles. On a POS (piece of sh**) bike? In four hours? The story was dubious at best. More likely a down right lie.

I picked him up and took him home. I don't think I even asked him about the truth. He would probably lie.

There's yet another bike story I just heard about the other day from Josh. Rick was riding his bike down Burkhart Street in Dayton, at the place where the first soap box derby was held. He accidently ran his bike into a parked car and got cited for speeding, Driving Under the Influence (DUI), and possession of an illegal substance. On a bicycle. As it turned out the officer wrote the citation wrong, so all the charges were dropped. And the city of Dayton got him a new bike, or so Josh just recently told me. I don't remember him getting a new bike. Maybe he kept it in a private garage with his '69 Corvette. He never had one of those either.

He also "borrowed" a horse one day, rode it through the Taco Bell drive through on Dayton-Xenia Road. With no saddle or bridle. Then he got it back into its pasture and let it run free again. No one the wiser for that excursion. I guess he really was a horse whisperer.

I didn't understand his recklessness, and desire to do adventurous, crazy things that just got worse and more dangerous the older he got. He and his friends would jump off railroad trellises into the Mad River. He just loved water activities. The riskier the adventure, the more he wanted to do it. One day he and some friends were jumping off the Huffman Dam outside of Fairborn, Ohio. That's a sixty-five-foot drop into a shallow, little creek. I imagine it was quite fun for the kids. Until one of the boys jumped, didn't get out quite far enough, and smashed against the wall of the dam. He didn't live to tell his story. Rick was a bit quieter for a while after that. He has never talked to me about the incident to this day.

Most of Rick's adventures were done with his best friend, Todd. Todd was an odd sort of fella in high school. He was a big guy, had a hardy laugh, and was good natured. If he'd get home from school and there was nobody there to stop him he would make a box of macaroni and cheese and have that with a bowl of instant mashed potatoes for a snack. He wasn't the smartest person I ever met, but his good nature and fun-loving spirit made up for that. I never really felt comfortable if he was over visiting Rick, and Sophie was there, with no adults around. Tragically, there was a fire in the middle of the night at his house. In the confusion and chaos his dad ran back in the house to get something, so Todd followed him in, shouting out his name in the smoke-filled bedroom. The firemen held him back. Todd heard his dad call out for him, just once. That was the last sound his dad ever made.

Josh never really seemed to like to talk to anyone much about the things he and Rick did during this era of their lives. So, I was surprised when not long ago he told me this story that took place in the mid-nineties when they were in high school:

"The day Rick painted the Confederate flag on the hood of the Dodge Aries, he was so proud of the job he did, he took me out to West Dayton to show it off. For some reason the locals didn't appreciate his art work, and shot the car, disabling it. While I was busy soiling myself, he went right up to the house of the guy who shot the car and used his phone to call a friend to tow it with a chain back to the house. But we only made it to Courthouse Square before being stopped by the police who told us we had to leave the car. Always thinking ahead, he was aware enough to realize it might not be a good idea for us to be sitting in a car that didn't really run at the time, with no brakes and bullet holes in it. We walked over to the Mead Tower and, after convincing the security guard that we had an appointment, we went to the top where we had a good view of the tow truck picking up the car. So, with all the foresight I can imagine anyone having, he had the car towed to his friend's house in Alpha." End of story.

Now Josh claims that was the longest day of his life—and all that happened before noon. I shudder to think about what else might have happened that day.

I remember that Dodge Aries. They got it from Joe's parents. The car had been parked in their backyard probably two or three years without being driven. The boys dug it out of a couple feet of snow and it started right up. They drove it home. Josh claimed that if he floored it, the car might get up to sixty miles per hour after traveling a full mile downhill with a strong tailwind. That made me feel like they had less of a chance of getting in trouble while they were driving around in it. There was no chance they could outrun anything. Also, the gear shifter thing was broke, so someone would have to get up under the hood to switch from neutral to reverse or drive. They had amended the device with a vice grip that was duct taped to some apparatus up under the hood. I was mortified when I saw the Confederate flag painted on it. He thought of it as a matter of freedom of speech. To me, it signified the ultimate in racism and discrimination. And I let Rick know in no uncertain terms that it had to go. My God, they could have been shot to death in high school. And I didn't even know about it till just now.

His troubles at school resulted in counseling...with multiple counselors. It turns out he could weave a good story with them, too. Like lying straight to their faces might be more accurate. They went for it, and affirmed he was okay a good kid with no psych issues. I still sometimes wonder what he might have told them about me, Joe, and our family situation. I'll bet it was interesting. And nowhere near reality.

* * * * *

During this time Joe was doing some fascinating work at Wright Patterson Air Force Base. It had to do with total quality management (TQM) initiatives. He was teaching classes to Air Force officers about better ways to manage their staff. A lot of people thought it was a crazy thing to try to implement. After all, officers traditionally manage by barking out orders, and expecting unquestioned adherence. The TQM system is embedded in the belief that every person in an organization must live up to the high standards of work that is expected in every aspect of its operations. The stuff he was teaching seemed to be just what we needed in our family, and I tried to get him to enact some of it at home. I guess he didn't have time. Or couldn't figure out how it would apply to us. Or maybe he just liked being at work more than he liked being with us some days. He sure spent a lot of time there.

In any event, I wasn't so sure his degree in psychology was of use to him when it came to raising his kids. And he spent more and more time traveling and "at work." I didn't like it, but there was nothing I could do. Joe said he was doing it all for us, because he loved us and wanted us to have a good life. Considering his long hours at work nearly every day, and continued travel, I wasn't so concerned about how much money he made. I wanted him at home and involved with me and our kids. That's what "a good life" meant to me. Eventually he said he would go where he felt most wanted. Apparently, that was at work. I tried to get us to move out in the country and back closer to where we grew up, thinking that it was the city life that I just couldn't deal with. We would also be closer to my family and I could visit them more often. But no, that wouldn't work. Joe had known someone from his home town who worked at Wright Patterson Air Force Base. He eventually rented a trailer closer to work, so he wouldn't have to drive back and forth sixty miles one way to work and back home every day. They ended up getting a divorce because he was gone from home so much of the time. Well I didn't want that. No way was I getting a divorce. So, I put up with his shenanigans and spending so much time at work. I later found out that the dude he knew from his home town ended up "stepping out" on his wife. Pretty sure it was that, and not the drive time to work and back, that was the cause of their divorce.

I thought about this conversation with Joe many times for years later. I wondered where he went for hours before and after his scheduled work time. I wondered if he held someone else in his arms when he travelled. He talked about how easy it would be to pick someone up while he was out of town—just go down to the bar and strike up a conversation with a lonely woman. I did end up getting multiple fungal infections, which didn't make sense to me. But I decided to not press him anymore on the subject. Joe never physically or verbally abused me. His pay check went straight in the bank. He took about $20 a week for lunches. Our marriage was solid. I was convinced. And yet I wondered...

⦿ ⦿ ⦿ ⦿ ⦿

Rick got a maintenance / lawn job at our church and learned a lot about planting flowers, etc. The priest was a bit obsessive about his flower garden. Rick said Father was so picky that he drew out a diagram of what he wanted planted and where it should grow. Then he would measure it after it was all planted, and make Rick move one flower if it was off by a centimeter from what Father had designed. I don't know, that might have been a bit of exaggeration. But I do know that one day Rick accidently clipped off a tulip. He was so scared that he would get yelled at, he decided to tape it back on. As far as I know, he got by with it. The fact that he was working for a slave driver priest seemed cool to me. Who gets in trouble working at church, right? Well, he was fired when one of his friends dropped off some pot, which Rick hid under a bench by the baseball field. Rick didn't understand that there might be something wrong with that. There were no little kids around to get into it at the time. He claimed the pot wasn't his. Why should he be in trouble? As it turns out, he was the last high school kid to work at that church. That makes sense, I guess.

On a summer morning after his junior year, I got up and discovered about a dozen high school boys sleeping all over the backyard, and in the living room. The trampoline had maybe three or four boys passed out on it. There was a truck in the driveway that I had never seen before. It had a big couch on it that looked like it had been partied on—hard. I was livid. I found Rick among the boys who made up the mosh pit in the living room and chewed him yet another new one. Most of the boys were from Tennessee. He had just met them the day before that. And they were at my house with my teenage daughter asleep in her room! What was he thinking? Nothing about him made any sense anymore. Where I smelled danger, he smelled adventure. And he loved adventure.

My hair was completely gray by then. And Rick hadn't yet graduated high school.

And this wasn't yet the worst of it.

One Monday morning in April of his senior year, I got up to go to work, and my car was gone. Rick was gone. I didn't even want to look for him—I figured that if he didn't want to be found, he wouldn't be found. So, I took Joe to work and then drove to work myself. I was fuming and worried all day. Where was Rick? What was he doing? The next day we got the car back. The police had found it stuck in the mud under a water tower a few miles from home. The only thing in it was a twelve pack of beer. Unopened. So where was Rick?

On Wednesday that same week we learned from the police that he and a girl had run off together. I got a call from the girl's dad who was a sheriff in eastern Ohio. Holy cow. A sheriff. I thought he'd be coming after us and put us away for Rick kidnapping his daughter. But no. He said he held his daughter totally responsible for them running off. She was always in trouble and running off with some boy or another. That eased my mind somewhat, even though the girl was fifteen, and Rick was eighteen. The dad was apologizing for his daughter running off with Rick. I dodged that bullet.

On Thursday of that same week I got a call from the police in Little Rock, Arkansas. Rick and the girl were arrested in a stolen car in a church parking lot. Apparently, they were doing the hokey pokey in the back seat when the police approached the car. By the time the police got in touch with me, the girl was in Children's

Services and her mom was on the way to go get her and take her back home. Rick was in jail. In *Little Rock, Arkansas!*

Joe, Josh, Sophie and I took off in the van the next day not knowing what to expect. Or even if we could get in to see him. We managed to hire a bail bondsman first thing in the morning. Funny how conveniently located bail bondsmen offices are to jails and court houses. He walked us across the street and over to the court house. He helped us get a lawyer. That was kind of interesting. We were in the lobby of the court house with the bail bondsman we hired, and he introduced us to a congressman who happened to be passing by. And happened to be a lawyer. What are the odds? We hired him on the spot. No contract. Just a handshake.

Then he took us over to the jail to help us get in to see Rick. Once there I was able to talk to a "lady", a very sullen, scary, solid, brick sh-house built kind of woman, the keeper of the jail gate, to let us visit Rick even though reservations were supposed to be made two days in advance (like he's going somewhere). It was horrifying waiting outside the tiny visitation room. There was an 8x11 inch window in the door I could peek through, into the room where we would soon be able to visit with him.

I could also see through the room and out into to three floors of the prison. There were prisoners of all shapes, sizes, and colors. They all looked like criminals, thugs, and derelicts. Not one of them looked like my son. He was my baby. My heart felt like it had dropped out of my chest. There was a lump in my throat the size of a watermelon. Was this happening? Could this be a real thing? Or was this just a dream? A myriad of other impossible questions raced through my brain. Was he safe? Could he sleep at night? How bad was the food? Was anyone hurting him? I couldn't stop the thoughts as I waited and waited to see my son.

Josh said he wanted to talk to him first. And alone. We all agreed. The two boys had been so close as kids. They could talk first. I saw Rick enter the tiny room in his orange jail bird suit.

I felt totally devoid of strength, and emotions. I forgot how to breathe. There was my son in chains. The two brothers spoke for a little while. Finally, I couldn't stand it another second. I opened the door, and went in. Josh had tears in his eyes. He looked betrayed and very sad. I don't know what happened in that room, but it seemed to me that nothing was ever the same between them after that. Josh seem to want nothing to do with Rick from then on.

Rick had a face of stone once I sat down across from him in the tiny meeting room. No real emotions. More ticked off than scared, or sorry. Almost like, "It's about time you got here. I'm ready to get out of this joint." Our fifteen-minute visit over was too soon. Joe, Josh and Sophie went to find a hotel. I stayed to talk to Rick some more as the jail lady had softened a bit and allowed me more time for another visit an hour later. She seemed to empathize with me when I explained we came from Ohio and were trying to arrange to get our son home. I got the distinct impression she wasn't accustomed to family coming hundreds of miles to get a prisoner out of jail.

So later that morning, I had some extended time alone with him in that tiny cubicle where prisoners sit with a thick glass between them and their family. The first thing I said was, "We haven't decided to take you home." He collapsed on the table. Now he looked scared. Maybe he didn't like his accommodations, or roomies after all. I told him we just couldn't have him be part of our family if he continued to do stuff like this. It was tearing us all apart. I didn't feel safe in my own home. I wanted to know why he ran off, and if he could change his ways; if he even wanted to change. He had no explanation. He didn't seem to think he even did something wrong. It left me feeling incredibly empty and I left.

We did bail him out the next day. It was a long, quiet, rainy ride home.

I called a family meeting after church on the following Sunday. Something nobody besides me ever seemed to like to do. It was very somber. The air felt thick. It was hard to speak. After a prayer, and some urging on, Rick said that he started using drugs when he was in third grade. I was aghast. He was eight years old in third grade. He explained that he would ride his bike to the park near our house and some high school kids would get him to deliver an envelope with something in it to this house or that one in the neighborhood. They would pay him. Eventually they paid him with cigarettes, and then pot. I felt sick. How could they do that? Getting my boy started on drugs—at age eight. Eight! This eventually led to him going as far as shooting up heroin behind the high school when he was a senior. He told us he shot it between his toes because it's harder to detect needle sticks there. I was beside myself as he told his story. All that drug activity was going on in my house and my neighborhood and I didn't have a clue about any of it. Druggies are sneaky.

Looking back on those early times now, I can recognize that there were strange, subtle changes in him. He would be dressed in the new day's school clothes in the morning when I woke him up, and he looked like he hadn't gotten any sleep. Because he hadn't. He explained that he was up delivering drugs for those bad boys in the middle of the night. I wanted to go after those kids who were dealing drugs right there in my neighborhood. I wanted to get the newspapers and TV stations and churches involved. I wanted everybody to know the terrible things that happened to my son. And I wanted them to make it stop. Immediately.

But I changed my mind when I began to consider how doing this could impact my other two kids. They would probably be targeted and ridiculed and bullied. They'd been through enough trauma because of him. So, I kept my mouth shut. From then on, I just wanted him to graduate high school and get the hell out of the house.

He made it through the graduation ceremony five weeks after we got back from Little Rock. I excitedly opened the folder with his diploma in it. Only there was no graduation diploma. Apparently, he owed money for a book, and he refused to pay it.

He claimed someone else had destroyed it, so he didn't feel like he should have to pay the bill. Well I wasn't going to pay it, so I still haven't seen his actual diploma. It was sad. And infuriating. He was so damn smart took college level courses like physics in high school. I thought he had a chance to get into medical school. Silly me. He received no high school diploma certificate because he owed $39 for a destroyed book. But…he was officially graduated. YAY!

CHAPTER 5

Rick's Early Adulthood

The troubles did not end with the completion of high school. Not by a long shot. Rick lived with his aunt in Celina for a while and had several different jobs while he was there. He worked at the garden center at Wal-Mart, and was a cook at Bob Evans, to name a couple. Legal issues followed him wherever he went. In one week, he had to be in court in Xenia, Celina, and Little Rock. It was all just more dumb stuff. Mostly traffic violations. One of the times when he had to go court in Xenia he realized he was thirsty and court wasn't open yet. He walked over to a gas station. He told me he didn't have enough money for a bottle of water. Instead he bought a can of beer, sat on the court house steps, and drank it. And got arrested. Off to jail he went. Did he have a working brain cell in his head?

So much of those years are just a blur. Forget about Rick going to college. He was crazy in love with a girl, Ashley, who dropped out of school, and had a history of using drugs—right along with her family. At least that's what Rick told me several times. Rick said he felt like he fit in with their family and lifestyle—he could smoke and drink and get stoned right along with them when he was visiting them. They felt more like family to him than we did, or so he said. Ashley seemed to like her pills and pot. And temper—whoo, baby, she had a temper and it would pop up at unpredictable times. We eventually heard she might have suffered some very traumatic things when she was a little girl. At one point, Rick said Ashley had been molested. And that could have contributed to her sudden mood swings, poor decision-making habits, and affinity for drugs. I don't know how I would have dealt with that myself.

One day she got mad when she was visiting Rick in Celina and hitched a ride with a trucker. Rick and I had to go after her. I still don't know how he knew what direction the trucker was headed in. We eventually caught up with her in Somerset, PA. We just happened to pull into a truck stop in the middle of the night and decided to get a little shut eye. I slept on a coffee table in a lounge area at the truck stop that night. I don't recommend it. In the morning, I struck up a conversation with someone who had worked there in the coffee shop area the day before. What a coincidence! According to our informant Ashley had some cuts and bruises and looked scared. The worker being very astute, assumed something bad had happened to her, and contacted the local emergency medical agency. They got her medical assistance and then she went with Children's Services—yes, she was still underage. The driver roughed Ashley up a bit and then must have realized that someone was on to him. He took off in his truck before the law could get there, leaving Ashley behind.

So, a Children's Services worker picked up Ashley. Our informant had no idea what might have happened to her after that. Rick was beside himself with anger over what we heard and wondered what condition she would be in when we found her. But he calmed down when we met her, her dad and uncle at Children's Services. We got to see her just as they were getting in the car to leave. She had some scrapes, cuts and bruises, but it wasn't nearly as bad as I imagined. She came up to me and quietly recommended that I not argue with her dad. Her dad said some not very nice things to me and Rick. I kept my trap shut, which was not easy to do.

Later that same day, once we got home, her dad called our house told me to stay out of their family issues. Then her uncle got on the phone and threatened to shoot my knees out if I caused them any trouble. If I caused them trouble? What the hell. I was trying to help. I told him I was a lady and would not tolerate him cussing me out like that. Surprisingly, he shut up. End of conversation. I did find myself looking over my shoulder now and then to check if the uncle was around the corner with a gun pointed at my knees.

* * * * *

A couple months later when Rick was twenty, Joe helped Rick and Ashley get an apartment; he paid the down payment and first month rent for their wedding gift. They didn't have two nickels to rub together but they were so in love. They believed their love would get them through anything. Oh, and did I mention that she was pregnant? Rick tried to make some quick money during this time by donating plasma. I couldn't even fathom that. But he tried to donate up to the allowable three times a week. At $25 a pop, that's $75 a week. Jackpot! But it wasn't enough to live on.

Several weeks after the wedding Rick was arrested for snatching a purse from an older lady in a grocery store parking lot. He tapped the woman on her shoulder as he grabbed her purse, so it was considered an assault. All of that for trying to get enough money to buy a bottle of Diet Coke for his bride. He ended up in jail. There were a lot of purse snatchings and assaults of older women in the Dayton area for about a year at the time. He made the front page of the Dayton paper. The paper was trying to bring attention to this purse snatching trend by making an example of him. The picture in the paper was him on a stretcher heading for the hospital. I recognized his hands on the top of the sheet before I saw his face. His hands always reminded me of Pop's hands; long perfect fingers, and very strong.

I went to the arraignment. Outside the court room there was a group of people in the hallway laughing and joking around. I assumed that the older woman in the group was the person Rick had assaulted. I walked up to her, introduced myself, and apologized to her for what Rick did and all she had to endure because of it. I explained that he was trying to get a Diet Coke for his pregnant wife who had a congenital medical issue with her esophagus. Diet Coke was the one thing that seemed to help the discomfort. There were three or four dudes hanging out with the woman and her daughter. They were carrying on like they were some kind of something.

The door to the court room opened and we all went in. I sat in the back and the dudes went up front. They were messing around, joking with the prosecutor, talking about how they were all that, and more. They had seen my son running through the back alley behind Robert's gun shop with the lady's purse the night of the incident in question, and they took him down. Hell, the prosecutor imagined out loud, he might have had a gun or even an Uzi or maybe a bazooka! All they had was an ax, but they were ready to put it in his head if he tried to fight them. He didn't. The prosecutor asked me if I was involved with the case. I said, "Yes, I'm the mother of the guy you think had an Uzi." The laughter stopped. You could hear a pin drop. I felt cold and empty inside.

Rick eventually walked into the courtroom—in hand cuffs, ankle chains, and yet another jail bird suit. Black and white striped this time. He looked translucent. He might have given too much plasma in the recent past. I swear I could almost see right through him. He went completely white and nearly tripped over his chains when he saw me. I just wanted to cry. I think I forgot how to breathe. Again. I don't even recall the details of what happened next, but it was soon over. I think the assault victim decided to not press charges as she wasn't hurt. And she now knew that Rick's wife was pregnant. He would still have to do jail time at some point. My cousin, Julie, was able to be with me at court that day. She gasped when she saw him. It was indeed a shock. I'm glad she was there. She helped me remember some the details of the event as my mind was blank when it was all over. I was pretty much in a stupor as I drove home.

Ashley ended up in the hospital while Rick was awaiting his arraignment. I guess she needed that Diet Coke bad. Some blood tests indicated the baby might have spina bifida, and the doctors and nurses talked to her about having an abortion. She was livid about that. And left the hospital against medical advice. I heard she ripped out her IV, got dressed and just left. Nobody was going to take her baby. She loved her baby.

I'm pretty sure the only two times Ashley went to see a doctor during her entire pregnancy were when I took her. Once, the fetal heart rate was 120; the other time it was in the 160s. I was a bit concerned about the extreme difference in pulse, but the doctor wasn't. Of course, she had no insurance so that might have contributed to the doctor's ambivalence. She got huge toward the end of the pregnancy—so big she didn't get out of the car when they would come over to visit.

Sophie tried to spend time with Ashley and seemed to provide emotional support. Ashley opened up to her and talked about how hard her life was. As a child, she got into drugs, was molested, and dropped out of school. And now as a teenager she was already pregnant. Sophie told me that Ashley was scared about becoming a mother at nineteen.

Josh was busy working during this time. He worked at a small grocery store, a Burger King, and Value City. It was a time he learned what kind of work he did not want to do once he got out of school. He also started dating Jess, who proved to be his soul-mate for life. He had no time to hang out with his brother. Or the rest of his family.

Then on a Sunday evening in August 1998 Rick called me and said Ashley had delivered. First a boy. Then a girl. Twins! That explained why the doctors thought the baby had spina bifida, and why she was so big. We rushed over to Mercy Hospital in Springfield. Hunter was born first. He looked like a little old man—he was so wrinkled up, and tiny. Riley was plump and vibrant. Throughout the labor, only one baby was anticipated.

But after Hunter came out and they were trying to remove the placenta, there appeared a little hand—Riley seeming to shout out, "Hey don't forget about me! Get me out of here too!" To this day she remains good at barking out orders!

Ashley tried so hard to be a good mom; she breast fed, and there would be no smoking around the babies once they were home. The first six weeks were doubly hard with having twins, oh and the fact that Rick had to spend those weekends in jail for the charges from the past year or so. So, Joe and I stayed with her and the twins every weekend. It's probably good they were twins. We would have argued over who got to hold the baby if there was just one.

When they were seven weeks old I got an urgent call. Ashley had awakened to a weak cough from Hunter and noticed a drop of blood on his nightie. She freaked out. They rushed him to the hospital, and while we were talking, Hunter was being helicoptered to Dayton Children's Hospital. We went there to wait for him.

Oh my God, I was shocked when he came in: that tiny baby on an adult sized stretcher with four or five medical staff working on him. His legs were a deep, dark purple color. I figured he would soon be dead, but if he survived he would certainly be a mess for the rest of his life. The next day I learned that if it had been another hour before he got medical attention, he would have died. He stayed in the hospital for a week—five days on a respirator—being treated for severe pneumonia.

The doctors instructed Rick and Ashley to give him breathing treatments four times a day. We were told that poor little baby would need them for the rest of his life. Amazingly, by the time he was ten months old he didn't need the treatments anymore. Ashley and Rick had taken such good care of him. He was cured. He was healthy. I was amazed.

Again, the memories are a blur. They lived in Fairborn for a while. Since they had no car, and neither of them had a driver's license, Rick rode a POS bike from their apartment in Fairborn, to a gardening company in Beavercreek, worked in the hot sun all day, then rode the bike back home. That must have been exhausting. Too bad they didn't make it easier on themselves by staying clear of drugs and away from the police.

Sophie tried her best to be a good aunt to the twins and sister-in-law to Ashley. She stopped by Rick and Ashley's house in Xenia as often as she could and helped them out as much as a high school girl was able. The stories she later told of times when Ashley would talk her into driving her around to "friends" houses in high crime areas of Dayton were quite disturbing. We didn't know it at the time, but as it turns out, this area of town is well known for illegal drug activity, and prostitution. They would make short stops. Ashley would run in a house for a few minutes, come back out, and away they'd go to the next stop. Except for this activity, Ashley seemed to be pretty much all together during much of this time frame. Motherhood seemed to suit her much better than I anticipated. She seemed happy when I was around her.

Rick was no saint during this time either. One night, Sophie took Ashley on one of her "rounds" and Sophie's boyfriend, Craig, stayed at the house with the twins. Craig later said that he thought Rick was locked in the basement the entire time. I have no doubt of it. It would be easy to lock someone down there if they went there for any reason—just close the trap door after them and lock it by putting a board through the handles. I figured Rick and Ashley had a fight and he went down for a little peace and quiet. We later found lots of empty beer cans all over the basement. I often wondered how much time he might have spent down there for "peace and quiet".

One day I went to check on them after work. I was accustomed to going in the house through the back door. There was a cryptic sign between the back door and kitchen door that read, "Don't take another step or you will be wacked on the head with a 2 x 4!" I have no words for that.

Joe and I continued to help by visiting and babysitting. It was not uncommon for us to take Hunter and Riley for what we expected to be a three or four-hour date night, and then not hear from Rick and Ashley for three or four days. We never got a reasonable explanation for their whereabouts during those times that made sense. It was exasperating.

❂ ❂ ❂ ❂ ❂

The twins were two the first time they were placed in foster care. What a shock that was! I felt shame, embarrassment, fear and anger all rolled into one. Why on earth could Rick and Ashley not take care of their kids? What it was like for Hunter and Riley I'll never know. They don't remember any of their first two years. Foster care seemed from the outside to be a good experience. They were treated equally with the other foster kids there. They were fed nutritious food and kept safe. There were rules and schedules, and the twins seemed to follow, and appreciate them. Each of the kids who lived with them there got a little square of carpet to sit on while they watched movies and ate popcorn on Friday nights. I think they liked having a piece of something that they could consider theirs alone, even if it was just a bit of carpet. Of course, if they had the opportunity, they would run from adults as fast as they could. It seemed so strange when they ran. They didn't seem to be running toward something and they didn't seem to be running away from anything. They just ran. Sometimes I would pick them up from the place they lived in Xenia and pass by a sod farm. Every time Riley saw it she would exclaim, "There's a running place, grandma!" I thought maybe it looked like freedom to her.

Their little brother Gunner was born the day after the twins turned five. I think that's how long Ashley's birth control implant was effective. I shudder to think how many kids they would have had if not for her birth control.

I didn't get to see Gunner till he was four months old. Probably because his mom and dad didn't like my opinion of their lack of appropriate parenting skills. Oh my, what a beautiful baby he was. Brown hair and eyes. Happy, smiling. And plump—I didn't have to question if he was fed. He was a joy, and his big brother and sister doted over him. Riley took up being the mom figure for him for several years. She made sure the diaper bag had everything in it that he would possibly need. She fed him and made sure he was clean and dry. It just seemed like Ashley was too tired to follow up on things like that which was understandable to a certain degree. Taking care of three pre-school kids is tiring. Been there. Done that.

At the time Gunner was born, Hunter and Riley had been homeless three times, and lived with three different foster care families. One of those times they were later placed with their Grandpa Joe for several months. Sophie was going to school into auto technology at Sinclair College during this time. She did as much as she could to help Joe with the kids. She even quit her job to help him, so Joe would be able to get to his job. I always thought she had so much strength of character, and this is just another example of it. Josh and Jess were married by this time and had lives of their own. Jess was so excited when she saw Gunner for the first time. She held him and squeezed him and loved him like he was her baby. Oh, how she giggled when she saw he sucked his thumb. From that day forward Gunner had a special place in Jess's heart.

* * * * *

I cannot imagine what this time of those kids' lives were like. Most kids I know would be excited to have a sleep over at some friend's, an uncle's or maybe grandma's. For them it was common to fall asleep in a house they had never been to before, surrounded by people who were probably stoned. And then wake up and wonder where they are. Frightening. So foster care seemed like a relatively good thing all things considered. At least they were safe, short term, with the same people day after day for several weeks. And the people were sober.

The emotional side of imagining what the day-to-day life of those kids was like during this time literally wore me out. I didn't sleep through the night. Ever. I worried about them having a roof over their heads. Even just looking at other little kids tore at my heart strings. It was painful to watch kids I didn't even know interact on playground equipment. My thoughts always went back to my grandkids and wondered if they were having the opportunity to have fun with other kids too. If they were safe or if they were even fed. Hunter would sometimes try to hide food from my house in his coat and pants pockets to take with him. That's a pretty good sign there wasn't much food in their house. He also rarely took off his coat. Even to sleep. Almost like he feared it would be gone by morning if he didn't wear it all night.

The whole thing was baffling to all of us. Sophie put it so well, "All Rick has to do is get up, go to work, then go home to take care of his family." She made it sound so simple. But of course, it wasn't simple. Nothing is simple when there's addiction and possible mental illness to contend with. What comes with it includes frustration, pain, confusion, denial and often total abject disbelief from the people who love them.

So finally, after years of watching my son circling the drain, the whole idea of acceptance that he was an addict and that I had already lost him to drugs, crept into my consciousness. As awful as it is to see a son and daughter-in-law sink deeper and deeper into the dark hole of drugs, it is even worse to realize that they would not, and could not, even try to overcome their problems. What I saw as total dysfunction and horror, they saw as their normal life. I'm sure they knew they struggled with their living situation, and yet they would choose to continue using drugs, losing jobs, and moving from town to town. It's what they did.

* * * * *

Rick and Ashley connected with some of her family who took them to some kind of fundamentalist church down by Cincinnati. I didn't take kindly to the whole notion of my son switching religions. Everybody was supposed to be Roman Catholic in order to attain eternal salvation. That's the way I was raised, and that's the way I wanted my kids to live as grown-ups. And yet I wanted to remain open-minded so Joe, Sophie and I went down there to attend a service.

Well, that was interesting. Sophie dressed up in what she thought was appropriate attire for church: a blouse, skirt, and a little make up with her hair down over her shoulders. We ended up sitting in the front row. That's something that Joe did that always made me crazy. He insisted on sitting in the front of any church we attended whether it was ours, or one we'd never been to before. I would have preferred to sit back farther that day, so we wouldn't be so obviously visiting.

We must have stuck out like a sore thumb. All the women in the congregation were kind of dull looking, no makeup, wearing floor length skirts and their hair up in a bun. Sophie was colorful, vibrant and had on a short skirt. She kept pulling it down over her knees, trying to make it look longer as we sat up there in the front row. I think some of the teenage girls were a bit jealous of her. She looked sexy. They didn't. They looked bored and boring. The sermon was all about the sin of temptation that women press upon men when they let their hair down, make up their face and allow their legs to show. I'm not sure if that was just a coincidence and the planned sermon of the day, or if the pastor took one look at us and switched things up a bit. We must have appeared as just down right scandalous heathens. Sophie was embarrassed to the moon and felt that all the adults there figured she was going to hell for dressing like that at church. Bottom line we didn't feel at all welcome and left without much socializing after the service.

Of course, Ashley was pregnant again.

CHAPTER 6

My Own Personal Hell

During this time in the new millennium, for all those years, I felt like I was barely treading water. Joe and I went through a legal dissolution of our marriage when Hunter and Riley were two. It was a very difficult decision. I never wanted to be divorced. Finally, I talked to our priest about it. I went in thinking I was going to get yelled at for not being enough of a woman to be a good wife to my man. I figured he would make it my fault that things were bad in our marriage to the point where Joe and I had grown apart. Instead he said simply, "The Church does not believe that God wants two people to stay in a marriage where there is no love." He added that if a partner strayed or love was lost, it was an indication that a real marriage commitment by that person was not made at the time of the marriage ceremony. Therefore, an annulment would be proper.

That was quite an eye-opener. And a relief. I did not feel the kind of love at that time that I remembered feeling through much of our marriage. I did not feel the special bond that I was certain that married couples would always feel. I'm sure we each did things that made us eventually aware that we were no longer the partners we'd planned to be. Perhaps we should not have been married in the first place. Joe was spending so much time doing work stuff with work people and told me several times he goes where he feels most wanted. Hmm. Guess that wasn't with me and the kids.

Being unmarried was something I never wanted, and it surprised nearly everyone when they found out, friends and family alike. Joe and I presented to everyone as a very together, loving, family-oriented, idyllic couple. The thing I openly give credit to Joe for is his adherence to the bible teaching that he continues to live by. Judge no one and, love everyone no matter who they are or what they do. That held us together for years. I tried to not judge him. I just loved him until I realized I didn't.

My sister Ginger was the first person I told. Her first response was, "Aren't you glad Mom and Pop aren't around to know about this?" I had thought of that. And I know divorce was not a possibility for me while they were alive. I wouldn't even recognize that things were bad between Joe and me till long after they were gone.

Josh and Sophie were probably the least surprised. They had been asking me nearly every week for the previous year if we were getting a divorce. They could tell that things were not okay between Joe and me. They each said they would be okay with this new norm. Josh was working and going to college, and Sophie was heading into her senior year of high school. Rick was out of the house by that time and had his own family, so he had no idea of what was going on with us. But when I told them, they cried with me.

I also got myself into ridiculous financial trouble with the IRS and some stupid real estate deals during this time. I mean, buying three houses in one year with the intention of flipping them and making big time money just as the housing bubble imploded, was very poor timing. To say the least. I was distraught, distressed, and close to death by suicide for several years. I really didn't know if I was more numb, crazy, or just plain absent from my true self. I lost probably $100,000 through all this. Not something a farm girl would routinely do or know how to deal with.

To top off that saga, we rented three of the houses because we couldn't sell them. For a while I was making four house payments, and sixteen utility payments a month. It sucked. I learned a lot about renters. Seldom did I find one who cared as much about the house as I did. One of them who was there for several years was actually pretty good. Her rent was paid through the county Metropolitan Housing Authority, so at least I got rent paid every month. The rest were mostly just plain unsavory. At least one of them had a meth lab in the upstairs kitchen which might have exploded. I heard different stories about it, so I'm not sure what the truth was. Josh found out about the lab when he went to collect rent, and the renter's face was scratched and scarred nearly to the bone. Apparently, meth makes some people feel like they have bugs crawling under their skin, and they try to remove them. Another man hanged himself in the attic. I wasn't allowed into the house to see where the hanging took place. I wanted to try to go in and figure out how to keep tenants out of the attic in the future to avoid future hangings. But the police said I couldn't enter the house unless the tenants gave me permission. They didn't.

Yet another tenant asked my permission to have a bird. I pictured a cute little canary in an ornate cage, singing sweetly in the morning. Silly me. His wife had a damn pet rooster. When I found out, I recalled how I killed and butchered chickens when I was I kid. It was tempting to find out if I still had those skills. They eventually kept about a dozen chickens in the basement. He and I argued over the definition of a bird. He said chickens are birds. I said they are livestock. He couldn't have livestock on my property. There were city ordinances that prohibit such activity. He'd have to get rid of them. It took a while, but he did. Then when he moved out, we discovered he'd left three to four inches of chicken poop in the back room of the basement. Ugh!

Add to that there were frozen, broken pipes that flooded the street out in front of another house that left about six inches of ice on Main Street. I had to tear out the kitchen floor and put in a new one after that. Leaky roofs seemed to happen when I was on my way to work so I'd have to climb up on the roof and cover it with a tarp as the monsoon continued. And of course, a furnace seemed to go out when it was three degrees outside and the tenants demanded it be fixed that night. Well, you get the picture.

So, combine my family issues with my personal issues, and it's fair to say I was a hot mess for quite a while. I don't know how I got through it. Apparently, my advice to other women who were living in stressful times was, "Just put your shoulders back, stick out your boobs and take one step after another in the direction they are pointed." It must have been good advice, as I got through all that. I'm not so sure I would follow it now as my boobs droop and pretty much just point south. I guess I'd be heading downhill all day if I followed that advice today. Maybe I should try wearing the rib brace I had when I was a kid and see if I can get them back up where they belong.

Some people who have known me my whole life will probably be surprised to read the above paragraphs. I didn't share much about those parts of my life with my extended family or friends. I was raised to keep a stiff upper lip, my mouth shut when it comes to personal issues, and fix my own problems. And as my brother Hank told my sister Ginger after out sister-in-law Dottie died, don't cry about death and stuff. I also realized there was really nothing any of them could or would be able to do to fix my problems. I never knew anyone who dealt with all the terrible stuff that was common place in my life. They didn't either. I had to figure out how to live with it and try to fix it on my own.

As far as my professional career went, that was not a money maker. Many things about being a nurse, I really appreciated. I liked interacting with patients, relieving their pain and helping them heal. I continue to marvel at the workings of the human body and realize that everything you put in it or do to it, is either good or bad for it. I didn't like the stench of cleaning out bedpans, or the stress of watching people die. So, I worked part time at a nursing home and made my way through Wright State University to become a social worker. When I landed my first job, I was stunned to be offered less than I was making as a nurse. Just

$8.50 an hour in 1987. I managed to get more than that before I started the job and accepted that I wasn't going to get rich at my new chosen profession.

The dynamics and excitement of working in a hospital always appealed to me more than the seemingly slower, more cumbersome pace I found in a nursing home. In a hospital I might need to see twenty patients a day, and most of them would be gone within a week. Some of their families I would know briefly. In a nursing home I would need to know up to a hundred-twenty residents. Not only that, I needed to understand their family dynamics and deal with some of them for years. Nursing homes are very complicated and the most regulated business in the US.

The whole process of dementia grabbed my attention early on. I eventually became a Certified Dementia Practitioner, and taught nursing home staff as well as the general public about dementia. As a result, I was called upon to do consulting in various other nursing homes where I helped the staff get a better handle on how to care for demented residents, and how to properly document on them. It was gratifying to walk into a nursing home for the first time, and as I looked through residents' charts see assessment documents I had created for another home. I suppose I worked in thirty different homes at different times.

I got involved with Greene County Council on Aging, which provides services for elderly in their homes. I was honored to be elected president of their Membership Committee. On a larger scale, I was named to the board of the Miami Valley Long Term Care Association which services eight counties with educational programs and valuable networking opportunities.

And just to stretch out my areas of expertise, I became a Certified Funeral Celebrant. That might sound like an odd thing to do, and most people don't understand it. I enjoyed finding out about an old person's life and documenting it when they came into a nursing home, so other staff would be able to better understand them. Likewise, I enjoy learning about the different aspects of a deceased person's life and talk about it in a way that helps their family and friends appreciate the life that just ended. I believe that I help the survivors through their grief process by the way I celebrate life during the funeral.

Of course, my life was not all work and no play throughout the early 2000's. Joe and I started playing darts while we were still married. I continued playing after we got the annulment. The better I got at it, the more I loved it. I played in both the Shaffer and Clark amusement venues; in the Dayton area and in several adjacent state tournaments, as well as international competitions in Chicago. For a while I played in several leagues and luck-of-the-draw competitions five evenings a week. For several years I was ranked in the top five female darters in the Dayton area.

As I was getting less accurate with my darts, and people were not engaging me to play on their team, my Strohs sister Sally was encouraging me to take up golf. My first reaction was "That's an old man's sport. Why would I want to do that?" She explained that it's something we could do into our eighties. So, I took up the game at age forty-nine. It has been a challenging, frustrating and at times funny experience. I have new friends through golf and have played in thirty-eight states. I'm so grateful Sally talked me into trying golf. It has helped me maintain focus and given me something fun to look forward to as I attempt to play golf in all fifty states.

Now back to Rick.

CHAPTER 7

Rick's Growing Family

By this time, with Ashley pregnant for the third time, Rick and Ashley had been working with social workers at Children's Services in four counties, and were then living in the Oxford, Ohio area. I was frantic in my desire to get the kids out of their situation and into somewhere, anywhere safe. I even felt that I could tolerate never seeing them again, if I knew they were in a safe, nurturing environment. They had been in foster care twice more. The last two times were with the same farm family outside of Germantown. All three kids seemed to prosper and develop there. The twins had some mood/behavior challenges. These are common conditions in families who have been through a lot of trauma, I came to understand. The farm family headed by Bruce and Bridgette was totally awesome. They took them in, nurtured them, loved them and gave them direction.

The boys adapted well. They loved being out on the farm. They got to drive some of the smaller vehicles. Riley, not so much. She would sometimes scream and fight when we dropped them off there. I mean she was near hysteria. Bridgette just took it all in and said she figured Riley missed her mom and that she would adjust once she felt safe with them. I hope that's all there was to it. I sometimes hated to leave once I dropped the kids off there. And yet all of us in our family had determined this was the best situation at the time. I kept hoping the kids would adjust and find some level of life satisfaction and peace there.

How Bruce and Bridgette managed to take in three foster kids amazed me. Bridgette figured that Rick and Ashley would be grateful to them for caring for their children when they were not able to. Instead, during visitations with the kids Ashley would tell them they didn't have to obey these adults. They didn't have to eat their food or do their chores. She wouldn't want to live there either, she told them. How ridiculous was that? It certainly didn't help with the adjustment process and it made things even more confusing for the kids.

And of course, the kids went back to Rick and Ashley each time they were in foster care. They would improve their behavior, get a job, pass home inspection through whichever Children's Services agency they were involved with at the time and say they were determined to be better parents. Unbelievable. And yet I can understand they would want their kids, and the kids would want to be with them. That's the way life should be. Kids should be with their parents. And their parents should be able to provide for them.

Fortunately, I guess, I had finally made a connection with Butler County Children's Service Worker, Tyna. She had alerted all the hospitals in the area surrounding Oxford to be on the look-out for someone meeting Ashley's description, who came in to deliver a baby. She requested they be checked for drugs, the mom and baby both.

So that's how I found out that little Katie was born—notification from a Children's Services agency. Katherine Christina. What a long name for such a tiny baby. A tiny baby who was subjected to the worst kind of abuse—malnourished, born with prescription drugs, street drugs and alcohol in her blood stream who was now my granddaughter. It just made me sick to realize what that baby already had been through. And yet I was so thrilled—my sixth grandchild was born. Hallelujah!!!

Since Tyna had already alerted the folks down there, proper blood tests were administered, and drug presence was proven. Katie had two blood transfusions to get the drugs out of her system. And then, dammit, she went home to her parents and siblings when she was two weeks old.

Now I'm certain they were all very happy to have her home. I can just imagine the giggles, and kids wanting to hold the baby. The absolute joy of a new baby in the house is undeniable. Two weeks later, another blood test and she was positive for four different types of drugs. This meant that Ashley was breast feeding Katie while using drugs. How cruel.

Katie was picked up from the hospital by the local Children's Services agency and delivered to my son and his wife, Josh and Jess, who welcomed her with open arms. This had been the plan. Months earlier, we all agreed to this, and preparations were made.

So much confusion followed. So many plans to prepare for this baby. She looked so frail that night. When she arrived at Josh and Jess's, her eyes were nearly matted shut. Tears dried to her little face. And she had such a weak, sad cry. She felt like a loose bag of marbles with no muscle control. I held her, and looked at her, and loved my little Katie. It was so wonderful that she could stay with our family.

Then came the meeting to determine the kids' ongoing living situation. Joe, his girlfriend (we had been divorced for two years by then), Sophie, Josh, Jess and I were there. Rick and Ashley showed up late. No surprise. On some level, it was more of a surprise they got there at all, as they lived so far away. This was the first time I'd seen them since way before Katie was born. I stood toe-to-toe with Rick and asked questions. How can you possibly be using drugs while your wife is pregnant or while she's breast feeding? And why can't you get your life together and take care of your family? I thought they were appropriate questions considering the circumstances. But he looked uncomfortable and didn't answer me. Their court appointed attorney instructed me to stand down.

I asked, "Are you saying I can't talk to my son?"

She said, "Yes, if he doesn't want to talk to you."

Rick said he didn't want to talk to me.

I sat down. Rick and Ashley laughed. What the hell?

The meeting started. Josh, Jess, Sophie, and I were not permitted to attend. Joe and his girlfriend were invited in, along with Rick and Ashley. What was that all about? Some thirty minutes later Rick and Ashley rushed out of the room, ran outside, and up the long driveway supposedly to their car which they said was parked on Main Street. Here she was, six weeks postpartum, and she was running a sprint with her shoes flying off her feet. Nothing was making sense that day, and there was more confusion to come as I watched them run toward where they said their ride was waiting. To this day I don't know what that was all about. I never heard if something spooked them in the meeting, or they just decided it was time to go. Like right now.

The director of Children's Services, Mr. Black, sat with me on the couch in the waiting room and proceeded to explain that the older three kids would go back to their parents as Joe and his girlfriend indicated they would be involved with the family, able to help financially, and with the care of the kids. Then he explained that all the drugs found in Katie's blood at the time of her birth, could possibly have been given during the labor and delivery process. It was a stretch for me, but I didn't try to dispute what he said about the pain, and anti-anxiety medications. And I told Mr. Black just that.

Then I looked him in the eye and said, "Mr. Black, I have never heard of women in labor getting marijuana in either pill or IV form during labor. Have you?" That was one of the drugs Ashley tested positive for at the time Katie was born.

Maybe he hadn't considered that I would question this insanity. He seemed taken aback. And the meeting was soon over. We all dispersed. The older three kids went back with their parents. Katie stayed with Josh and Jess.

* * * * *

What a busy, happy, but frustrating time. Katie was happy and growing, as she quickly adapted to living with a different mommy-aunt, daddy-uncle, and cousins-brother/sister. Josh and Jess had remodeled the upstairs bedroom and Katie had her own little space. She quickly adjusted from the uncertainty of being unsafe and insecure and not properly cared for to always having people present who could provide for her every need. I was so happy to get to keep her overnight on weekends. I had no contact with Rick or Ashley, except for supervised visits at Children's Services in Hamilton.

It seems like Hunter, Riley and Gunner were back with Bruce and Bridgette in Germantown by this time. We carted them down to visit with their parents on weekends. Reunification with the family of origin is the ultimate goal of Children's Services, no matter how dysfunctional and messed up the parents are, and how loving and able the rest of the family is. That was tough to deal with. We tried to provide the kids with what they needed: food, nurturing, love, safety, security, and fun—"normal" living for kids. Conversely, at each visit, Rick and Ashley gave them more candy than kids should have in a whole year and the identity of being their mommy and daddy. What a choice. Of course, kids want to be with their parents. No matter what the parents are like. No matter if they are physically, emotionally, or psychologically able to provide for their kids. No matter if the kids are abused. They want to be with their parents.

I don't know how Josh and Jess got through this time. They had their own family, and financial struggles. Now Jess was working with Children's Services in Greene, Montgomery, Butler, and Hamilton Counties, picking up cheese and milk from Women Infants and Children (WIC) services. Trying to make ends meet— on many levels. And she had to allow for Ashley to spend time with Katie. Sometimes this was twice a week. Josh and Jess so wanted Ashley to be able to take Katie back into her own family. Josh wasn't all that thrilled to take in his brother's daughter in the first place. Yet he proved to be a fantastic dad to her. We all were hanging in there taking care of this baby while her dad was out doing...who knows what. It was awful all around.

* * * * *

Time went on and the stresses in my family continued to explode, both individually and within my family. All of us adults had jobs and did what we could to support Rick and Ashley's kids. None of us knew what Rick and Ashley were doing because they were basically AWOL. But we all knew they weren't present to take care of their kids. I didn't even know where they were living most of the time, if they were together, or if they were even alive. I did know that with every new thing that happened, every time those four kids were subjected to additional pain, rejection, or confusion, I felt like my heart was again jerked out of my chest and kicked around the block a time or two. Just for some sick kind of fun for somebody.

Finally, I looked up the probate judge who oversaw the Butler County Children's Services. The judge had six or seven objectives which described expectations of staff to obtain best outcomes for the children under their care. The whole thing looked like a lie considering what we'd experienced. The guardian ad litem assigned to the kids was ridiculous. I just could not wrap my head around the fact they identified the best thing for the kids was to be with their parents in sometimes horrifying situations that put them all at risk. And I didn't even know how bad it was at the time. If their parents were able to provide safety and security for their kids, I'd be all about reunification. Clearly this was not the case. I wrote the judge a letter, by email and snail mail, reporting to him how his staff had violated each of his stated objectives regarding my grandchildren. All three kids were shortly thereafter released from their parents' custody and placed with their Grandpa Joe. Those objectives disappeared from the website the next time I checked.

And then, a whole new set of dominoes began to fall.

CHAPTER 8

New Living Situations

Joe's life certainly changed literally overnight. He had been single for several years, and now had nine-year-old twins and a four-year-old in his house 24/7. Plus, he had a very high-status government job and had to travel sometimes. I don't know how he did it, but I did hear him say several times that he gained a whole new appreciation for the single parents he knew over the years. It just occurred to me that he may have lost some decibels of hearing during those years. It had to have gotten loud in that house with those very lively kids. And, he now wears hearing aids.

I was in the habit of keeping a variety of grandkids overnight most every weekend. I had to laugh one Saturday morning, when Sophie stopped by, and six kids ran out the door to greet her. Her eyes bugged out in disbelief and she said, "How can you do that? Six kids!"

I just grinned and told her about all the fun we had: making a fort in the basement out of the furniture and blankets, stuffing shirts and pants with balloons then playing bumper kids till someone started to cry, chasing each other around in the house in figure eights through the kitchen, living room and bedrooms. And of course, we had to have popcorn with pop juice (lemonlime pop and berry juice). I loved having the kids over and would have done it more except I was working a full-time job and did consulting on weekends at six places. Frequently, I would work five or six weeks straight with just one or two days off. That was my attempt to reconcile the above referenced financial hell I put myself in.

One Saturday night in April 2009 I had Katie, who was then nearly three and Riley, then age ten, over for the night. We had just watched a movie about a dog who got separated from his family, then reconnected with them. Katie was already asleep in the playpen. Riley was brushing her teeth when the phone rang. It was Grandpa Joe. He had just gotten a call from Ashley's dad. Ashley was staying with him in southeastern Ohio for the weekend. I heard he was working on a two-story addition to his house trailer at the time. Anyway, he went out to see what Ashley was up to, as she had been sitting in the front yard and leaning up against a tree for a good bit. She was dead. He carried her body in the house. As it turned out Ashley had experimented with mixing some drugs together to try to get a different kind of high. Instead she got a fatal combination. Not what she wanted to do. She loved her kids and wanted to get them back. Or at least see them grow up.

Her death changed everything for the kids. Again.

Joe asked me to help him tell the kids. He seemed to not know what to do. Or how to talk to them about this. I went into the bedroom where Riley had just lay down. I lay down next to her and said, "Riley I have some very bad news."

Riley asked, "What?"

"Your Mommy died today."

We cried for about ten minutes. She lifted her head and asked very defiantly as if someone lied to me, "Who told you that?"

"Grandpa."

We cried a little longer, and then she told me I should leave the room. I said she could come in my room if she wanted. Or I could come back and stay with her later if she didn't want to be alone. She didn't want either one of those options. She slept alone that night with her little sister in the playpen next to her. Riley never talked to me about that night. I can't imagine the grief and pain she felt. Her mom was dead. She didn't know where her dad was. I couldn't imagine anything worse than that.

The funeral was odd. Gunner and Riley quietly and without anyone noticing, walked up to the casket. Just the two of them. When I saw them there, their little silhouettes against a vast casket that held their mommy, I rushed up and put an arm around each of them. Riley quietly sobbed, her shoulders shaking. Gunner looked confused and rattled. He didn't cry or speak. He was five. Their mom lay dead in a box. How do children deal with that? They just stood there looking at her for a few minutes. Then they slowly turned, walked around to Joe and Hunter and sat down in chairs that seemed almost too big for them. No child should have to experience that and live with the memory for the rest of their lives.

I talked for a bit with the pastor of their church in Cincinnati. The same one who gave the sermon about the importance of women not forcing men to lust based on how they dressed. He remarked that she looked like she had been through some tough situations. My mouth took off without my brain in gear, and I said I noticed at recent funerals that the bodies looked rough, and I figured that it was because the trend was to make death look more real by not putting on so much makeup. He said, "Well, she looks really, really dead." The fact is the drugs she used changed the composition of her blood, so her face and neck swelled up.

Several of Ashley's family spoke. Her dad rambled on till his mom interrupted him. I stayed clear of the uncle who threatened to shoot my knees out several years before. Her brother committed himself to finishing up Ashley's children's books. Well that was a surprise—I wasn't convinced that she could read and now I find out that she'd been penning books. I wonder if he ever got them done.

None of us in Ohio knew where Rick was at the time of Ashley's death. It had been several years since I'd seen him or heard from him. Word was that he left Ashley at some point before she died. As it turns out, a body can't be cremated or buried without the consent of the person's living spouse, unless a diligent search has been concluded, and the whereabouts of the spouse continues to be unknown. We had come to believe that he was in Dry Gulch, Kentucky as he mailed the kids occasional birthday and holiday cards with a post mark from there. Notices were placed in area newspapers—around Dayton and Dry Gulch. After six weeks, there was no response.

So, per the direction of Ashley's dad and her grandma, her body was cremated weeks after the viewing. Finally, Ashley's cremains could be put to rest. Joe was asked to pick up the ashes. Keep in mind that his life was hellishly, frantically busy with those three kids under his roof and his full-time job. Now he had his daughter-in-law's ashes in his van. It gave me the creeps, but I had to peek at them. There they were in the back of Joe's van, going everywhere he went with the kids. The ashes seemed to be packed with care—the box was inside a maroon velvet bag with a gold braid tied around the opening. Very respectful, I thought. But still, ashes. I couldn't force myself to open the bag to look inside.

A few days later, Joe got the call to deliver the ashes to the cemetery. I didn't know any of this was going on until I noticed I had a voice mail message on my phone at work. It was from Joe. He sounded very harried, stressed out. "I'm leaving the cemetery now. We tried to pour the ashes into the urn. The wind picked up, so we put the whole bag in it. It just figures that Ashley would spend all of eternity in a baggie." That sounded awful to me at the time, but later I realized that's the way things are done with ashes.

Katie's future was now uncertain. Josh and Jess had intended to keep her until Rick and Ashley were cleaned up, off drugs and could take her back for good. This had happened before; Rick and Ashley were able to get jobs, be drug free, and live in acceptable places in the past so they could get their kids back. Josh and Jess hoped it would happen again. And it would be permanent. Clearly that was not an option now. Joe, Sophie and I all tried to figure out how we could take Katie in. I was checking into babysitting arrangements with my neighbors and signing her up for private school at Ascension Church. It was a painful time. We all wanted her to have a good life. We all loved her. We all knew she needed a mommy and daddy who would love her as their own.

As it turns out, Sophie worked with someone whose nephew, Chris, had been trying to adopt a baby for three years. They'd had several unsuccessful attempts at in vitro fertilization. Their hope was to get a three-year-old or younger girl to adopt. Could this be the answer? The couple was from the Dayton area. What are the chances of that? Chris and his wife, Melissa, started to visit with Katie, and take her to their home for weekend visits. Eventually they decided to adopt her. It just seemed like Katie belonged with them. They wanted to have a closed adoption—no one from our family was to try to contact her in any way. Ever. It broke my heart to think that the best thing for my Katie was to let someone else raise her, and as a result I'd probably never see her again.

Katie and Riley stayed overnight with me on that Memorial Day weekend in 2009. Katie would move in with Chris and Melissa the following Thursday. Katie always called me Grumma, her way of saying Grandma. It would prove to be the last day I would spend with her. We went swimming at the local Recreation Center. At one point, Katie watched as a young woman who looked remarkably like her mommy, got out of the pool and walked past us to go over and sit in her beach chair. She was followed by her two little boys who separately went to her, hugged her, and said "I love you, Mommy." Katie got out of the water, walked toward the woman and with her arms outstretched said, "I love you Mommy." It was the most natural thing in the world for her to do. A little girl wants to be with her mommy.

My heart was breaking for her as my eyes filled with tears. It was then that I embraced the belief that Katie was born to Rick and Ashley to be raised by Chris and Melissa. I just can't accept the concept in most situations that something happened because "it was meant to be." Every decision made in life has options;

sometimes we choose the one that has a good outcome—sometimes we goof and choose the one that leaves us with still more challenges to deal with. But I do believe that in this case the love and power of God brought Katie to her new family, so she would be the daughter of a couple she hadn't met till a few months earlier. And have a better chance at a wonderful life than she would if she stayed with us, her natural family. This, I will continue to believe through all my days. And I hope that there will be enough time in years to come when Katie and I can really get to know each other again. My motto became: "Katie, always loved, never forgotten."

CHAPTER 9

Continuing Chaos

Certain chaotic uncertainty is about the best I can do right now to sum up the ensuing several years. Three kids who had been through some incredible, unpredictable, horrendous situations, still loved their mommy. And she was dead. We had no idea where their dad was. Could he be dead, as well?

Fortunately, they had been with Grandpa Joe for several years, and felt some sense of security with him. The counseling services continued. Grandpa tried so hard to get their lives into some level of normalcy. He got them involved with every sport they showed an interest in—softball, football, cheer leading, karate, basketball, wrestling, volleyball and he coached them in the ones he could. I stayed as involved as I was able, transporting them places, watching games, going to Parent Teacher Organization meetings, taking them to church, having them stay over on weekends with their cousins. I even coached their volleyball and softball teams.

Although I disagreed with Joe on some of his disciplining/ parenting practices (or seemingly lack thereof!), I will always be grateful for all that he did for them. He kept them as safe as he could and fed them and was there for them. Every day. He indeed has been a hero to those kids. At one point I remember him talking about getting other foster kids when his grandkids moved out. The whole thing was turning out to be easier than he ever expected. I chuckled when he said that, but he seemed serious. Things really were going very well, and Joe was glad he took the kids into his home and dedicated his life to them.

And then the twins collided with eighth grade. And all hell broke out.

Riley was going to church in a "Little Kentucky" area of Fairborn. She found it herself and felt good about going there every Wednesday and Sunday. She was baptized in the church before I knew she was even going to it. She was very involved in the youth group and helped whenever she could. They had spaghetti dinners for the congregation, which the kids cooked. Some of it was edible. She helped with setting up Sunday school for the little ones. I took her to the services and activities sometimes, though it wasn't easy for me to think she wanted to be there.

The neighborhood looked like most people had ongoing garage sales, like daily...lots of items (junk) in their yards. Cats lazily roamed the streets with their tails sashaying side to side seeming to try to attract the local tomcats, and chickens pecked in the yards and on the streets trying to get a morsel of food, cackling to each other as they went.

When I went to a Sunday service for the first time, I was greeted by a man who asked if I was a sister. I said, 'No, I'm Riley's grandma." He looked at me like I was weird, probably not suspecting I felt that way about him. I realized as the words were coming out of my mouth that he was asking if I was a sister in the Lord. My response was to inform him that I was not a nun. Oh well you can't get things right all the time.

I went to a Sunday service to see what the church was all about. The women all wore long skirts and had their hair tied up in a bun. Dang. This might be the same kind of church their mom and dad got involved with. I was glad I had on long, big pants, and a loose-fitting shirt with a collar that went clear up to my chin. I didn't want to be the subject of the sermon here. The service was pretty alright, the singing was awesome. Those folks could play a tune on their guitars, banjos, organ, piano, and drums. I was truly impressed with their musical abilities. The average age of the folks there in the church proper was probably around seventy-two. The kids had their own separate Sunday school service.

The main event came towards the end of the service. The children came into the main part of church and settled in. They sat in the pew in front of me. Since I went without Joe, I sat in the back row. I noticed the fella who greeted me before the service began, had earlier stepped out the back door. At the proper signal, he came rushing back in, when it seemed like the service was nearly over. He ran up the center aisle, all wrapped up in a gush of energy, praising the Lord in loud bursts of adoration. He got up on stage and the power of the spirit literally brought him to tears, as he sobbed and tried to bring that same spirit into the poor wretched souls there in the church that day. My eyebrows were up along my hair line in wonderment. I just don't get into that kind of worship service. I guess the spirit missed my soul that day. I was one of the few there who wasn't crying and beating my chest with my fist. It wore me out just watching the whole deal. To me it seemed more like a stage production than a Sunday homily. And the congregation was expected to be fully involved with the show by raising their hands up to the heavens and shouting out loud, "Amen!" to indicate they fully agreed with the preacher. I still shake my head in disbelief just thinking about it.

Riley just happened to get interested in that church at the same time she got interested in boys. She was fourteen after all. What a mess. She got kicked out of the local roller-skating rink, when she was caught making out with some of the boys from the church group in the back room. I guess some girls just go through that type of thing as a rite of passage.

About that same time, Riley stayed over at my house with some assortment of cousins. Since her phone was dead, she used my phone to check her Facebook page. She then forgot to log out of her account on my phone. So, the next week I was getting fifty to a hundred Facebook posts a day from her friends, some with interesting pictures. Clearly her friends did not know they were on Facebook with Riley's grandma, or they wouldn't be posting some very personal stuff. I couldn't get in touch with her because her phone was still dead. That Friday I stopped by their house. I handed her my phone and said, "Would you please make it, so your Facebook posts don't come to my phone?"

The shocked expression on her face was priceless, and she shouted out, "That's impossible. You can't be getting in my Facebook account!" She was getting close to hysteria.

I very calmly said, "Well I don't know how it's happening, but Dallas wants to make out with you and you think just a kiss would be enough. And Cameron looks really hot with his shirt off."

She grabbed my phone with a harrumph, and shortly thereafter gave it back. As far as I know, she never checked her Facebook posts on my phone again. I was surprised when she asked me that night if I wanted her to delete her Facebook account. I paused to consider my words. "I think that some of the stuff you and others post is inappropriate, unnecessary, and offensive. It could even lead you into trouble. But I won't be able to stop you from getting on it. I just hope you're careful." Besides, I knew she could start a new one and we wouldn't know anything about it or be able to monitor it. I added that it was between her and grandpa.

Hunter continued to struggle with his emotions, and odd decision-making habits. He wanted to stay with his cousins on Ashley's side of the family for sleep overs. I'll never forget the time he proudly stated, "Grandma, I went dumpster diving for the first time last night!"

Now I try hard to not go nuts when I hear something like that because I want them to feel comfortable talking to me about anything they do, no matter how far out I think it is or if it's illegal. So, we talked about what the experience was like for him, and what kind of stuff he found in the dumpsters. What I really wanted to do was shake some sense into him. My grandson was dumpster-diving and thought it was cool. How mortifying.

Another time he was out with them, he got stopped by the cashier for picking up a cigarette lighter at a convenience store. Apparently, it's illegal for anyone under the age of eighteen to buy a cigarette lighter, so even picking one up will get a fella in trouble. I'll never know if that happened, as he denied that he was planning to shop lift it. He was so scared of disappointing Grandpa because the police were involved, that he threatened to kill himself. That's when I got the call from Joe to meet Hunter in the emergency department at Kettering Hospital. What was left of my heart sank when I saw my fourteen-year-old grandson being escorted by the police into the hospital in leather restraints. That was a long night. We talked about a lot of meaningless stuff, and what happened at the convenience store. He was very clear to me that he had no intention of hurting himself. The reason he said what he said was because, he didn't want Grandpa to know the police were involved. He didn't want to disappoint Grandpa. It was just sad. He was okay in the morning and was released from ER. I took him home. We never again talked about that night.

So, one day Hunter and Riley made plans to run away from home while they were in the dugout at a softball game I was coaching. This was still the summer of their eighth grade. They packed their backpacks and left the house in the middle of the night. Apparently, they got to the end of the cul-de-sac, looked at each other and didn't know where to go or what to do next. So, they just started walking. Joe realized they were gone once he got up. He immediately started an all out search. He called the police and some of the kids on the softball team. He followed the twins trail very accurately. I was very impressed that he would get to a place shortly after they had just left it.

I stopped by Joe's house after I got off work. He was talking on the phone to Ashley's sister. She wanted to know if Joe could pick up the kids. They had told her that Joe said they could be there, and they had been at her apartment most of the day.

Joe said he'd go get them. What? He would go get them? I said he didn't have to go get them. They found their way there; they could find their own way home or take a ride home in the squad car. Joe agreed. And that's what happened. Joe got the police to agree to take them home.

When I heard they were on their way home, I went to my house and got ready for their softball game—I was the coach of their team, after all. When I returned to his house on my way to the game, I got a quick update from Joe. They were not in just the greatest state of mind when they got home in the back of a squad car. They knew they were in trouble yet seemed glad to be home—they had walked a lot in the past fifteen hours. And their aunt let the kids and Joe know she was pissed that the police came instead of Joe. What a mess.

I was so glad they were safe, and hoped they learned a meaningful lesson from their actions of the day. I decided to go upstairs and offer them support and consolation to help them get through what must have been a scary night and day. I figured it would be inappropriate for me to do what I thought about doing, which was kicking their asses for causing Joe and me to worry about them all day. Riley was hysterical, crying and asking why I wouldn't let her play on the team. Hunter was the same. What? I wanted to get into why they decided to run away from home in the middle of the night, and they were concerned about not being allowed to play softball!

The decibel level was getting high. Riley was in her room. Joe seemed to have gotten Hunter under control, so I went to the game. I stopped by the house again after the game. Things had not exactly stayed under control from earlier. Joe had a concussion and needed stitches. Hunter somehow ended up with a two-foot length of PCV pipe in his hand and whacked Joe with it. He was removed from the house by the police. He didn't remember a thing about hurting Joe.

Eventually all that worked out. Hunter might have spent some time in juvie for hurting Joe. It's hard to remember the details. But things were always so messed up. Joe, being the calm responsible person, took Hunter back. And life went on as usual.

I don't know what might have been going on in Gunner's mind through his young childhood. Mostly he learned to pacify himself, first by sucking his thumb as a baby, and rubbing a silky blanket or cloth. Kind of like I did as a kid. Then as he got older he'd just stay out of the way when tempers flared. He rarely initiated turmoil yet often was the subject and recipient of his brother's flare ups. And he did have some instances when his temper flared, and he struck out at someone.

Of course, I don't know how I would handle it if I was a kid in a similar situation and some other jack ass kid came up to me and said something like, "I'm glad your mom is dead, so she doesn't have to see what you're turning into." I'd probably want to punch them in the throat too.

Gunner continued to keep a low profile into his middle school years during all the crazy escapades of his siblings. He sometimes accompanied them when they did some dumb stuff that got them in trouble with the law, but he generally got off scot-free. Probably because he was so young and so damn cute. Once they thought it was fun to blow up firecrackers in an empty construction truck behind the grade school. Must have been loud as many neighbors complained. The twins had to do some community service. I don't think Gunner got in any trouble. Probably since he is so much younger than them. Rather than playing sports like the twins did, Gunner stayed in Scouts longer than they did. He did try wrestling but didn't really like the idea of grabbing and hugging a boy he'd never even seen before. Also, he wasn't crazy about wearing the wrestling singlet. I can't say I disagree. It was form fitting. He seemed to be choosing good friends through all this and didn't get into trouble. I just wished he could express himself about all the crap he has had to deal with in his young life.

One thing all three kids shared when they were in grade school and middle school, was being unable to handle it when they were in an emotional situation. Good or bad. None of them wanted to be hugged or even touched on the arm or shoulder. Chances are if someone tried to show them affection or comfort unexpectedly, they would end up with a knuckle sandwich. On the other hand, if one of them was the subject of harsh criticism from a coach or teacher, they would clam up and withdraw into themselves. Nearly to the point of being catatonic, unresponsive. If the situation persisted, often they would erupt into rage. Man is that scary to watch! There were times when one of them would tear up a room, like a classroom if their teacher was showing them unwelcomed, individual attention. They would throw things around the room and out in the hall. Then physically and emotionally spent when the tantrum was over, they were passive and swore they didn't do it. How could they not remember doing such a thing? I did some research and learned this condition is called Reactive Attachment Disorder (RAD) and is common in abused children and /or children who have been taken away from their parents. Fortunately, they have managed to overcome these emotional disturbances. They allow me to hug them and they hug me back. They even tell me they love me. It's fantastic to see them mature.

CHAPTER 10

Getting Older, Finding Rick

Those years when the twins were into their teens were just more insane chaos. The kids and Joe were down right creative with the frenzied lifestyle they lived. It almost seemed normal, or at least doable. For them. I probably would have done things a little differently. Eating habits would have included more home-cooked meals; less junk food. There would have been fewer friends coming and going, day and night, without even knocking on the door. Electronics would have been put away when they went to bed. At least that's what I think I would have done. Joe did things his way. And it seemed to work well overall. He kept them safe and fed. He kept them in school. He protected them. In many ways he was a hero to them. He is a hero to me.

Sometimes I felt like I had nowhere to turn for support, understanding, and acceptance. Especially when a new trauma presented itself. I felt lost and alone. I didn't know anyone who had lived with the horrors of addiction like I was experiencing: grandparents doing what they could to provide a decent life for three of their grandkids, another grandchild living in another town with another family, their mom dead, and their dad nowhere to be found. No one in my circle of family and friends was able to understand what I was living or feel my confusion and pain. It was easier to just not talk about it.

I continued to go to counseling and Al-Anon meetings now and then, to help come to grips with some of the rougher patches I was going through. The main thing I got from doing that was to the realize that I just can't fix everything. And sometimes I can't fix anything. It left me feeling lost and more alone in my own world. But at least I finally came to understand that other normal people live alone in crazy worlds, too. The other thing I got, mostly from Al-Anon participation, is the importance of detaching yourself from the person who is addicted to drugs or alcohol. That's hard to do. Especially when you think someone you love could be killing themselves by these habits. But I realized I had distanced myself from Rick six years earlier. At the time it seemed more painful to see him and what he was doing to himself and his kids than to not see him at all.

My sister, Ginger, was always there prodding me on to talk about what was happening. Urging me be open and talk about some terrible things going on in my family that I treated as just another thing for me. I was never sure she could comprehend on an emotional level what I was going through. She deals with things more on a logical basis. It's different to consider hardships on a wholly logical level when there's so much emotional turmoil wrapped up in them. Especially when it's your family. Of course, she had dealt with family crises of her husband's death and raising her three boys by herself. She did one heck of good job with them. They are each a wonderful son to Ginger, brothers to each other, and phenomenal dads to their own kids. She is indeed blessed.

Frances, my sister who is two years older than me, lived far away in Alaska. There were times when we talked that she and her husband, Vic, helped me understand things on a very deep emotional level. They were just awesome. Of all my siblings, she sees life more through emotions than the rest. Most of the others are logical thinkers, like Ginger. Sometimes I just need someone to be emotional with me because that's the way things can make more sense to me and fit into place. At times logic makes me feel dumb, because my life isn't at all logical. But generally, when Frances and I talked, I tried to keep things light-hearted and live vicariously through the stories of her life. She lives out in the mountains and wilderness. It helped me a lot to just imagine being there. Free of all the insanity of my life. She was always there for me in spirit, even if she couldn't be present and involved with my life on a day-to-day basis.

The rest of my family knew very little of what was going on. In some ways it was easier to not talk about it with them. Their lives were so different from mine. Their kids were pretty much grown and had wonderful, amazing families of their own. Comparatively, my life sucked.

Some of my friends were very supportive. I don't know what I would have done without the time and support of my best friend Sally. We met in first grade and have been good friends all these years. She is also a Strohs Sister. We did everything together; driving tractors, dating boys, nursing school, softball, and eventually golf. We even got married the same year. When I told her I was going to get a divorce, she said she would, too, because "We do everything together." And she did. Of course, she had her own reasons for getting divorced. She has been my confidante, mentor, counselor and friend throughout our adult lives. She helped me figure things out and decide what to do. I don't know what I would have done or would do without her ongoing support.

I mentioned earlier I felt like I was just treading water. That's saying a lot for me to be able to tread water because me and water don't get along very well. This might be related to us not having a shower in the tub when I was a kid. We could put just enough water in the bath tub, so the bottom was covered. Seems like we washed our hair in the sink, so we didn't use a lot of water and Mom wouldn't have to regenerate it so often. I can swim now but for most of my life I would freak out if I was in water over my navel. Finally, in this imaginary scenario which seemed to invade my consciousness for years, I decided to try to reach land. And what do you know? It seemed like the water was only up to my chest, not up over my head and I could walk right out. What a relief to realize I wouldn't have to work so hard to just breathe.

And I could move around on dry land as I please. Once I imagined that, I decided it was time to get things right with Rick.

● ● ● ● ●

Coincidently, as I was yearning more than usual to see my son Rick, Joe got a letter from him. I was about to turn sixty and I hadn't seen nor heard from him in over six years. That's ten percent of my life, and nearly twenty percent of Rick's life. Joe called me to let me know about it. I went over to his house and got the letter from him. Tears filled my eyes as I read it. It was a long letter, hand written. In it Rick described how he had accomplished all the things Joe said he had to do before he could visit with his kids again: have a steady job, no legal problems, no debt, a stable address and phone number. For four years he had maintained a life with no drug use. Reading it was like getting a breath of fresh air after being in a musty old cave all day. Zippity doo dah, what a wonderful day! It was quite a relief to know he was finally getting his life together. And it was so exciting I wanted to laugh, and sing, and dance. Everything sounded so good. There was no malice, or blaming, or anger. He just wanted to see his kids. He wrote his phone number down towards the end of the letter.

I couldn't stand it. I called the number. It went straight to voice mail. I tried to text. I called again. He answered. What joy, I heard his voice. "Hello."

I said, "Rick?"

He said, "Yes. Who is this?"

I said, "Your mother."

There was a long pause. I think we each had to take a breath and catch up with what was happening. We cautiously talked.

Then he said, "Wait a minute. Who are you really? Is this a prank? When is my birthday?"

I told him, and added my birthdate, and just blabbered all kinds of stuff he knew only I would know.

He stopped me, "Okay, okay! Now I believe you. At first you sounded like one your sisters." We talked for quite a while, most of it reliving crazy memories of many years ago. And we agreed to meet the next Sunday at the Riverscape in Dayton. I still wasn't sure I could trust him; he put me through so much hell. But I didn't want to be sixty years old without having seen my son again.

I waited at Riverscape for Rick. Joe found out we'd made arrangements to meet, so he planned to get the kids out there, a while later. That way I would have a chance to spend some time alone with Rick. And the kids could spend the rest of the afternoon with him. I was sitting there looking out at the river and I could feel him softly saunter up behind me.

"Mom." I turned to see him. He was hesitant, yet grinning from ear to ear.

We hugged and cried and laughed and hugged and cried and laughed. My God he was so strong, healthy, happy, and handsome. He told me he had helped build Riverscape pavilion and went into detail about what he did which was mostly concrete work. He also had been keeping up with Joe and the kids from a distance. He had been by their house and sometimes actually got to see them. But he didn't approach them. He was waiting to be invited back into our family, and yet scared he wouldn't be accepted. Our visit was short. Joe and the kids were on their way to meet Rick.

That reunion was totally awesome. Tenuous at first, though with big hugs. Rick wrapped his big, strong arms around all of them at once. There was so much happiness there, it seemed like the moment could go on forever and not one of us would care if the world missed us. After a short visit, the kids took off with their dad, and Joe followed them. They were going to get some food and just…be together. My son was back in my life, and I felt alive for the first time in…well I don't know how long. Things were finally going to be good in our family.

I wanted to see for myself where and how he lived, so I made plans to go out to his house the next weekend. Sophie caught wind of this and called to try to talk me out of going by myself. She said she could only think about the night when she was sitting in a car with Ashley on the street out in front of our house. She was petrified, thinking that Rick was inside murdering me, and she was scared to go into the house and check. A plethora of similar incidents rushed through my mind. That boy put me through so much hell. But I wanted to see him. And see what his life was about. So, I calmly said I didn't think he'd kill me that week-end. She chuckled and said that since I put it that way, maybe he wouldn't murder me. I will admit I felt a bit uncomfortable about going alone, but nobody volunteered to go with me. It's strange to think about feeling uneasy about seeing your own son. Josh didn't say a thing about it. He still didn't want to have anything to do with Rick.

The place was easy to find—just a two-and-a-half-hour drive from my house to his. He had a small apartment on the first floor of what had been a funeral home. It was probably built in the late-1800s. It smelled funny, but it was very clean. Ammonia-smelling clean. I think it was mostly just the furniture that was malodorous—like animals had done the nasty on it, or worse. But I won't go into that. There wasn't much besides beer in his fridge. That was okay with me. I like beer. We talked and talked and talked. We drove around, and he showed me several houses and barns he had built in the area. He showed me places he shopped, bought his groceries, and where he got parts for his car. Such a simple day. And yet, it was totally awesome to be there with my son. Driving around in my car with my son beside me for the first time in twenty years.

I admit, though, Sophie's words were reverberating in my head when we went out to his friend's place in a very remote area. I mean, two-tire-track gravel road remote. He wanted to show me a three-story deer stand he had built just a half mile out in those woods. "This is where he's going to do it", the thought rattled through my head. Nobody would find my body till hunting season. Dammit why did Sophie have to say what she said? The stand, as it turned out, was very well built. We climbed up in it and I got a whole new perspective on the hunting thing. And then we walked away. Gracious sakes. I felt like I dodged a bullet that never existed. We walked past the turkey barn he had built, and I verified that turkey poop is the worst smelling crap I have ever experienced. It cleared my sinuses. It even made me dizzy.

We stopped at several places in town, and I was amazed that everybody knew him. They called him Bucko and he really seemed well known and well respected wherever he went. He had to do some work on his friend, Lois's van, so we walked over there. Lois seemed like a very gregarious, fun-loving, outspoken kind of person. I immediately liked her. She was Rick's best friend, and probably the person who saved his life when he was at his very worst with drugs. They were just getting started with piloting big loads over long distances on highways. I could hardly believe his words when he told me that's what he was doing. He had a job driving and had to drive a car with flashing lights on top. He couldn't even keep a driver's license in Ohio! And often back then, he rode in the backseat of a car with flashing lights on top while a cop piloted the car. Now he was telling cops where they would have to drive. And they did what he said—without question. What a transition. He was a survivor, and I loved it.

That night they were scheduled to do karaoke at the local Fraternal Order of Eagles Lodge. Yep they did karaoke, not only at the Eagles, but they were in high demand for weddings, etc. They didn't have exactly the most high-tech equipment. I think they might have gotten some of the TV screens from different dumpsters around town. But they figured out how to make it work. And it worked very well. That night was so much fun. Just like during the day, everybody knew Rick. I noticed that some folks were asking him about how he felt, and they were glad he was out of the hospital. Hmmm? I wondered what that was all about.

The Rose, by Bette Midler came up and the person who sang it was awesome. Every note she sang was on key and she put such feeling into it. Rick knew it was one of my favorite songs. It immediately took me back to the day so long ago when he hired the acapella choir to sing it to me when he was in junior high. Rick got me on the dance floor. We held each other in our arms. We smiled while our tears gushed down our faces. We clutched each other like I'm sure no thirty-five-year-old man and his sixty-year-old mom ever did before. I felt so lucky to be able to hold him and love him. We held on to each other through the break between that song and the next which was a slow song, too. Tears were streaming off my chin as I got back to reality. I was getting reacquainted with my son. Lois was running the music. She was crying as hard as we were. I love that woman. Such a kindred spirit she is!

The next big surprise of the night was watching Rick sing his standard song at his karaoke gigs *"Gloom Despair and Agony on Me"* from the movie *O Brother Where Art Thou?* (Released 2000 by Touchstone Pictures) That was a treat. It was absolutely the funniest thing I ever saw him do. I would have never expected over the course of his life to that point that he would sing in front of people. Dang, he was good and so entertaining.

The event was over way too soon. We loaded up all the equipment and headed home. Rick and I sat up and talked some more way into the wee hours of the morning. We caught up with so much. I asked why so many people said something about him being safe and out of the hospital. He explained that about two months earlier, he was eating a bacon cheese-burger from a local restaurant. Suddenly he stopped breathing and was unresponsive. His friend since junior high, Todd, was there. Todd called 911 and started CPR. Rick was rushed to the hospital and ended up on a respirator for four days. It was touch-and-go for a while, but he finally emerged from what he was told was an allergic reaction to bacon and could return home. That incident was the impetus for his writing the letter to Joe about wanting to see his kids. He had looked death in the eye again and wanted to make things right with his family.

Wow, what a night. I was breathing the same air as Rick. It was so wonderful. Finally, we were so tired we couldn't talk anymore. He went to his room, and I got comfortable on the couch. We drifted off to sleep. Early in the morning, I got up to use the toilet. I was about to pass his bedroom and decided to peek in. He looked so peaceful lying there asleep. I couldn't resist being closer to him, so I lay down on top of the covers next to him. The past thirty-five years slipped away, and he was my little baby again. I cherished every breath I saw him take. I wish every mother could be as close to their grown kids as I was with Rick that night. I wanted to hold him and love him forever. Then reality came back to me. He was a big man now. I couldn't hold him like I did when he was a baby. He eventually opened his eyes, saw me and said, "Hey you!" Then he got up and we started on our new day.

That day being Sunday, we went to church services. He was very active in his church. He was head usher and had remodeled much of the interior into separate classrooms for the kids to have their Sunday school classes. It was amazing to see the work he'd done there, and watch people interact with him. I learned he had gotten several of the parishioners off drugs, and he would make sure they got to church on Sundays, too. I continued to be very impressed with his current lifestyle. The service was totally awesome. I didn't even mind that it wasn't Catholic. The sermon covered aspects of forgiveness, love for everyone, and the importance of not judging others. Same as Joe's strength in faith. I agreed afterward with Rick that it seemed like the pastor was talking directly to him and me individually. Lois and some other people I met the night before were at the service. I was very much looking forward to being more involved there and getting to know these fun, hard-working folks. And I had my chance now. Yay me!

The day was too soon done. I knew I had to leave, yet I wanted to stay. I wanted to belong there. I planned to do what I could to be part of this place. Did I mention I got my son back? After six years of not knowing if he was even alive, I could see him, and talk to him, and touch him. It was one of the best days of my life.

Over the course of the next three years or so, we kept I-75 pretty flat going back and forth to Dry Gulch nearly every weekend. Sometimes I'd stay down there. Sometimes the kids and/or Joe would stay. Man, it was great. When it was nice weather, we would have a campfire in his backyard. That's where I got to know and love Rick all over again and got answers to some of the nagging questions that really bothered me over the years. He talked about his deep love for Ashley. How he didn't think he would ever be able to fall in love again. How he continued to put on his wedding ring every anniversary since her death. How he even kept his ring considering all the moves and crap he'd been through surpassed my comprehension.

He gave me more details about his early drug use. He again described how he shot heroin up in between his toes way back in high school—in the woods behind the building. He admitted to smoking a lot of pot and did a bunch of cocaine. When I asked him why he did all that, he merely stated he didn't know. He knew it was dumb and wrong, and he just did it anyway. Now he wished he had never gotten involved with drugs. He admitted that he wasted eighteen years of his life because of drugs. And he had nothing to show for it. He didn't even have his kids. And he hoped to high heaven that none of his kids ever used drugs.

I asked him why he couldn't keep a job back in Ohio, and why they moved around so much. He explained they were into drugs from the time they first met right on through making babies and eventually being separated from them. Sometimes one or the other of them would try to stop using, but that attempt soon ended, and they would both be using again. Drugs were their life at the time. Along with that, Ashley had a very hard time taking care of the kids by herself when Rick was out of the house. If Rick got up for work and she would wake up, she would beg him to stay home with her. And if he insisted on leaving, she would threaten to kill the kids and then herself before he got home. Sometimes he would get up at four in the morning, so he could sneak out to work without waking her up. He always came home to welcoming kids and a pissed off wife. Then he would try to make sure the kids had what they needed like food, and family fun time—and appease his wife with love and affection.

Rick went into more detail about Ashley's drug use early in their lives together, like when the twins were very little. He said he knew Ashley got Sophie to take her to places in the Dayton area for the express purpose of getting drugs. He felt so bad about it when he described how hard his life had been as we sat and talked in his backyard, but he didn't know how to change it back then. He talked about how he would get a call in the middle of the night from some stranger telling him to come get her because she had passed out, and even sometimes overdosed on whatever she ingested. He couldn't recall the number of times he would go into a place where she had ended up, find her unconscious, and need to do CPR. Lots of those times there were drugs and money all over the place, and little kids amongst it all. Sooo scary. And through it all he loved Ashley like a crazy man.

He realized that Ashley had some mental health issues. The more he thought back on this, he more he wondered if the mental illness lead her to the drug abuse as she tried to self-medicate, or if the drug abuse made the mental illness worse. We concurred that it was a vicious cycle; the more drugs she used, the more emotionally unstable she became. He noted that when she was clean from drugs she was very involved with their kids. She was loving and interacted well with everyone. But then she'd go back to them. The urge was just too great. And the cycle continued.

He had quite a story about how he got to Dry Gulch the town where he was currently living. He felt like his kids were stolen from him. Yep, stolen. Never mind all the drugs, the car accidents, and moves, and no money, no home, no food; he felt the kids were stolen from him. They moved to a small town in Kentucky after Hunter, Riley, and Gunner were with Joe, and Katie was with Josh and Jess. He and Ashley fought quite a bit. Finally, one day he realized that he absolutely could not stay with her. As much as he wanted to love her and protect her, he knew it was a bad situation and getting worse. So, he got on his bike (another POS) and rode it till he couldn't go anymore. He was exhausted. Finally, he ended up at a drop off area for furniture, clothes and books. It was the middle of the night. There was a couch there, so he got under the pillows and slept. He kept his hand on his bike out from under the couch pillow, so he would wake up if anybody tried to take it.

That's exactly what happened. Someone tried to look at the bike and Rick jumped out and started yelling. I'm not sure who was more surprised, him or the other fella. They got to talking. Rick told him about his life, and his troubles. The fella said, "I've been where you are." He left it at that and drove away. A little while later he came back with a loaf of bread, a pound of bologna and a quart of milk. He told Rick that when he was ready to get clean, to look him up. He could and would help him make a new start.

That was the beginning of Rick's redemption from the clutches of the drug demons. Rick later connected with this fella. Sam was his name. They become quick and lifelong friends. Sam did indeed help Rick get clean. He got him a place to live, and work. That was another lucky break, Sam owned a construction outfit, and Rick could work with him right away. With Rick's experience in construction, he could handle any job Sam had for him. So that's how that happened.

Rick claimed he sent birthday and holiday cards to all three kids regularly. He even located where Katie lived and sent stuff to her new address. This seemed weird because Joe would get one or two cards at a time for the kids, but never three. I have no idea about any of that, if it happened, or where the mail went. And I sure don't know if Katie ever got anything.

It was kind of weird spending time with Eric's friend Todd again. He had a truck driving job several years before this. He was in a major traffic accident while he was on the job and ended up losing his left leg. That pretty much took care of his driving job. One good thing was that he got a sizable monetary settlement from the guy who caused the accident. The bad thing about that was he blew most of it on partying. Rick talked him into getting a huge Dodge Ram truck with the last little bit that was left. I don't even want to think about what all might have gone down in that machine. It was a thing of beauty at one time.

* * * * *

About a year into us getting together again, Rick moved out into a two-bedroom house in a small town, Happy Hills. I referred to it as BFE (Bum Fu** Egypt) since it was truly in the middle of nowhere. He wanted to get his kids back and figured that he would need to have more room for them. The plan started to fall into place. Hunter moved in with Rick as soon as he could. He had very little adjustment problems starting in a new school. He got a job in a lumber company within weeks of getting there. Good God, I couldn't believe the transformation in that boy. He went from not wanting to do anything besides playing games on his computer to riding dirt bikes and four-wheelers all over the place. In no time, he decided computer games were a dumb waste of time, and he started working on engines. It was something to see. He was happy.

Gunner also considered moving there. He and Grandpa Joe were always so close. Joe was his father figure for nearly his whole life. He just couldn't make up his mind those first years. Maybe later. That's a tough decision. He hadn't seen his dad since he was three. Should he move in with a man whom he never really knew? Or stay with his grandpa where he felt safe? He decided to keep his options open and stay with Joe for now. He also really got into the bikes and four-wheelers. Those two boys were getting good at taking things apart and tearing up the yard.

I enjoyed riding the four-wheelers myself. I even threw Rick off the back end when I was driving a great big one. That thing had some power. Maybe I should have let up on the clutch a little more gently. He never let me take the driver's seat or control the throttle again.

Riley, as it turns out, was the person who had been pursuing Rick on Facebook for months before we all got reconnected. They had been talking on Facebook regularly for several months before they got to meet. Once they all got back together, she could not find happiness in the situation at all. What it finally came down to was that the boys got their dad back, but she would never get her mom back. I guess it didn't register with her that she had her dad back too, and the boys would never have their mom back either. It seemed to leave her with a chip on her shoulder that she just couldn't knock off. Altercations continued amongst all of them.

Riley continued to get more and more unpredictable, even though she was getting counseling five days a week. Somehow, she got things from friends she maybe should not have had. She experimented with drugs and alcohol. It seemed like once she started, she could not stop. But it made her feel better when she was high. She saw absolutely nothing wrong with using pot. She didn't even consider it a drug. It made her feel less anxious, more relaxed. The tall wooden privacy fence around Grandpa's backyard was accessible from her bedroom window, and I'm pretty sure she figured out how to get out and down to the ground without anyone in the house knowing a thing about it. She could play for a while with her friends in the middle of the night. Then climb back in her room before sun up, no one the wiser.

She told me she considered cutting herself on her arms intentionally with knives—to release her inner anxiety and pain. I've met other people who have done that. It seems so odd. Why would someone hurt themselves on purpose? As it turns out, I learned many of them have lived through so much physical/emotional trauma that is all bottled up inside them. They don't know why it feels good to them, somehow, to have a fresh cut and watch as the blood (pain) releases and gets washed away. At times it seemed like she was on an emotional roller coaster ride.

Eventually it was determined by Children's Services and the court system that she would have to go to a residential treatment center in Toledo. Rick and Joe took her up there. I can't even imagine what that was like. I mean most of the girls there were from the local Toledo area. The few times I visited her, I didn't see any other white kids, not that it made any difference. Just not what she was used to. She gets along with just about anyone. Some of the girls made advances to her, she got in fights and held her own. Every one of her teachers and counselors, talked about how much spunk she had and how they believed she would make it in life once she got out. She stayed for about nine months and was released. Joe and I went up to Toledo together to pick her up and get her home. On the way home, she talked and talked about how she was going to finish high school, become an electrician, and do everything she could to have a great life. She had no interest in doing drugs or hanging out with people who would get her in trouble. All she wanted to do was get a good education and then a good job.

Well so much for that idea. A few months later, Joe was working at the Moose Lodge when he got a call from the Secret Service. They were at his house and wanted to get in. He told them Gunner was home alone, and please wait till he got there. Sure enough, the black Suburbans with blackened windows were parked in front of his house. The G-men in black suits greeted him as they got out of their cars. They asked if they could search his house for a printer. He said he had nothing to hide so they could go ahead. They found a printer that Joe said Riley's boyfriend had recently brought in the house. They took it, and Joe's printer as well.

Then they looked around for more questionable items. Jackpot! They found a box with some unusual paper in it. Riley's boyfriend had been busy. He found a way to buy things without working somewhere to get a pay check. Instead he just made his own money.

If it wasn't so horrific, it would have been hilarious. I mean, who does that?

CHAPTER 11

Daisy Enters the Picture

Rick being a man, and finally feeling good about himself and life in general, was ready to be in a relationship. Daisy had just been through a terrible divorce and was in the mood to meet someone who would sweep her off her feet. She did not have a whole lot of self-confidence. Who does when you get a divorce from a man who Daisy described to me as mean as a snake, and treats you like crap? She had lost a lot of weight during that process, and now looked thin, yet healthy and happy.

Rick and Daisy spotted each other at Wal-Mart. She eyeballed him first. "Wow what a hunk of a man he is!" she thought. "He's so tall and strong and handsome." Dare she take a chance and approach him? Clarise was with her. They had been best friends their whole lives. Clarise was the more out-going, risk-taker of the two. She convinced Daisy to make a move.

I'm pretty sure it was love at first sight. There was a definite connection. I later met Daisy at a dance at the Eagles where Rick and his friend Lois were providing the Karaoke music and enter-tainment. I danced and danced with Rick and Daisy. Daisy seemed to be just right for Rick. She was so friendly, nice, and had the biggest smile of anyone in the whole world. Especially when she looked at Rick. And Clarise, well she was just downright fun to be around. My heart started to swell with happiness. My family was coming together, and I was liking the process. There were more campfires to enjoy in the backyard and so many more conversations to share. We even played softball in the open field beyond Rick's yard. I just knew everything was going to continue to get better.

Not only did my family seem to be healing and recovering, it might get bigger soon, if we could all just get along.

Sophie and Josh didn't feel the same way. Sophie kept saying she would be part of any family gathering that Rick attended, but no way would she reach out to him. She had no plans to go visit him. Josh wouldn't even talk about him, nor did he want to hear anything about him. He referred to him as the golden boy. This hurt. I never thought that any of them were better than the other two kids. I loved them equally. My fears about the impact of Rick's behaviors going way back to junior high school years were real. That stupid stuff he did really did impact his younger brother and sister and the way they felt about him.

Rick accepted that Josh and Sophie weren't so keen on the idea of him being a part of the family again. The prodigal son returns home, but not everyone is happy about it. Rick figured it would just take time till they would come around. He knew he'd been awful to them, so he was willing to take it slow. He hoped that once he got the kids back, Sophie and Josh would trust him and want him back in their lives. I was so looking forward to being one big happy family again!

It just made me smile all day long.

Once they had been together about a year or so, Rick surprised Daisy by planning a trip to Mexico. She was so excited, she couldn't sit still when they stopped by Joe's the night before they left. She was silly, giddy and ever so happy all rolled into one. She'd never been anywhere before. I don't think she'd even been out of Kentucky. The setting was perfect the night he proposed. They were in the swimming pool at the condo where they were staying. The moon was up high in the crystal-clear sky. Their favorite song was playing. He popped the question. I would have loved to hear the scream that came out of her mouth—the sheer ecstasy of the moment. They found each other. They fell in love. And their love would last forever, until death do they part.

Rick told Joe before they left for Mexico that he was going to propose to Daisy. Joe and I talked about the situation and how things had changed in the past three years. We were so glad Rick was back with us, and we each admitted out loud for the first time that we hoped that they waited till the kids were through school before they got married, or even moved in with each other. The kids were doing so well when they were first reconnected with their dad. Then as Rick got closer to Daisy and her family, he was drifting further away from his kids again. Like there was a developing wedge between him and them. Again. It was getting really frustrating for all of us. Sure, we were happy Rick found someone who made him feel alive for the first time in a decade. But we thought his kids should get first dibs on him. They needed him. Seemed to Joe and me like Daisy could wait. But holy hell he was happy!

They found a place out in the country. A couple acres. An old farm house completely upgraded. And a barn that was astonishing. The beauty of the hand-hewn rafters, and braces. All walnut wood. They were going to get married in it. It needed a lot of work before that day came.

I went up to help with cleaning out the barn several weekends in the spring. I loved it there. I loved cleaning out the upper floor of the barn. I loved seeing how Rick had figured out how to get water out of the crawl space under the barn by putting the sump pump inside an upside-down laundry basket to keep it from getting clogged by all the debris mixed in with the muddy water. I loved seeing how happy he was.

I was walking around in the barn yard with Rick one Saturday morning in early April and he asked me if I remembered what I said when he asked what I thought of his apartment, the one in the old funeral home. I couldn't remember. He recalled I said I never imagined him living in a place like that. Once he said it, I did remember that I made that statement.

I took a long slow look at the house, the barn, all the space in between and all the space for as far as I could see. I said, "I do remember saying that. This is where I imagined you living for the rest of your life."

That was such a happy day.

That was also the day that he asked if I thought was be a good idea to put an outhouse over by the side of the barn. I had thought about that. The barn is quite a distance from the house and, well, when you gotta go, you gotta go! Plus, Daisy insisted that people take off their shoes when they go in the house which took even more time till you could relieve yourself. He quickly added that Daisy was totally against it. But he surmised he could win her over by making it a flush outhouse. I questioned him a little bit about how that could work. Would he run water out there? What would he flush it into? He said that he had no clue as to how to go about making that happen, but he would figure it out. I totally believed him. He was always so creative when it came to doing the impossible. Probably the result would have something to do with duct tape and a vice grip or popsicle sticks, I chuckled out loud as we seriously discussed it.

Rick also talked about how much progress he thought he and Josh were making towards getting closer. They had already talked on the phone several times. He dreamed of the day he and Josh would sit and talk in the barn. That sounded so sweet. I hadn't heard from Josh that they were talking on the phone and planning to get together before the wedding. I hoped it was true.

By this time there was a noticeable rift between Rick's kids and Daisy's family. It seemed like Rick's kids felt he was rejecting them. Again. Oh, how I wished they could wait to get married till at least Hunter and Riley were through high school. Daisy's family welcomed Rick with open arms. So, while her family was getting close to Rick, Rick's kids felt like they were losing their dad. Again. I heard Daisy say that they tried to keep his kids close and help them feel part of her family. I believed her. I still do. Unfortunately, the more Rick enjoyed time with her family, the more his kids felt left out of his life. It got to the point where his kids did not want to be around their dad much. Possibly part of the problem was it was hard to get a time with him when Daisy and/or some of her family were not in the mix. It sucked for Rick's kids. And yet Rick and Daisy were crazy in love, and I was happy for them.

I took Riley and Gunner out to spend some time out there on Mother's Day weekend. It was also the weekend of Daisy's daughter's prom. Amanda was gorgeous. Her hair and makeup perfect. I wondered what was going on in Riley's head as she sat in the kitchen while all the festivities went on, all about Amanda. Riley missed her each of her proms because of the choices she made.

It was a chilly, rainy day which seemed to set the mood for the kids. Gunner refused to get out of the car. He was mad about something and wouldn't even talk about it. Rick tried to interact with him. No go.

Hunter was on his way out to the place Rick now called home. He and Amanda had been close friends till Rick and Daisy decided to get hitched. His friends teased him about his relationship with his step-sister. He didn't think it was funny. It was just another reason to be bitter. He brought papers for Rick to sign so he could join the Army Reserves that summer. Hunter was seventeen and needed his dad's permission to join the military. They never did get around to taking care of the paper work.

Rick, Daisy, Riley and I were out in the workshop just hanging out till the weather cleared. I was surprised at all of the tools and other equipment he had for working on vehicles. It was like a full-service garage. He talked about how he had gotten the giant, wheeled tool boxes on sale here and there and how he enjoyed having Hunter and Gunner along as he worked on his collection. He got tools for them as well. He planned to have a side job of working on cars in his shop and would teach his boys the craft. I estimated he had $20,000 of equipment there. At one point while we were in the shop, Rick smacked Daisy on the ass and giggled as he glanced over at me and said, "I love that woman!" They were fun to watch.

Hunter eventually arrived. When he came out to the workshop, Gunner finally got out of the car and joined the rest of us there. Sharp words were spoken between Rick and Hunter. Then the three kids took off with Hunter's friend. It would turn out to be the last time the five of us would be together under the same roof.

*   *   *   *   *

The following week I started looking for a proper dress to wear for their wedding. I wanted something kind of earthy, yet a little elegant. Something just right for the mother of the happy groom. I tried on a dress that was a wrap around and was supposed to cross over in the front. The dress was probably three or four sizes too small and did not close in the front the way it was designed to. The cleavage went way down to my naval. It was so funny I took a picture of what I saw in the mirror, and texted it to Daisy, hoping she'd get a good laugh from it too.

CHAPTER 12

The Dominoes Fall

So, about two o'clock on a Tuesday afternoon in late May 2016, Rick posted a video clip on Facebook. He was standing on the pool deck in his backyard and talking about how nice it was to have the week off to work on the homestead in preparation for their wedding which would take place there in sixty days. He continued to say that he should be mowing the lawn, or working in the house, but instead he wanted to jump in the pool. He dived in, got out and said, "Sometimes you just gotta circulate the water." He picked up his can of beer and sat on a lawn chair. The chair immediately collapsed under his weight. He said, "Dang it". Then he took a sip of beer, got up and turned off the camera.

* * * * *

I played golf that afternoon in Springfield. My phone rang. It was Daisy. I just knew she wanted to talk about the picture of the dress I sent her. I hoped she thought it was funny. Clearly, I couldn't talk then. I was playing golf. And she continued to call. Then I got calls from other numbers in her same area code. I got to thinking that maybe she didn't like the dress after all. In fact, she must be ticked off that I would even send her such a revealing picture of myself. And when she showed it to other people they got mad too and wanted to give me their two cents worth. I turned off my phone. I would call her after golf was done and apologize.

After golf, I was putting my clubs in the trunk of my car and looking forward to having a sandwich and adult beverage with my friends. The phone rang again. It was Daisy's brother calling

113

to say there had been a swimming pool accident, and Rick was hurt bad. Something else he said lead me to believe he was dead, but I don't remember exactly what it was.

I turned to Dave who was in my league and putting his clubs in his car next to me. I said, "I just found out my son died. Please tell them inside."

I felt like a robot as I got into my car to make the two-and-a-half-hour drive to see my son who was now apparently dead. I felt my chest intermittently swelling and shrinking. I guess it would be called breathing. It just felt so different. It hurt to breathe. My lungs felt on fire. It was hard to suck in air and release it again. I had driven that same route so many times in the past three years, why was it taking so long this time?

I called some of my friends, and siblings to let them know. I called Joe. Joe said he was told to bring the kids. I tried to explain that only happens when there's a death. He couldn't wrap his head around it. Even when I said, "Joe, Rick is dead."

It seemed to take an eternity to get to the hospital. So many people were calling to get an update, which I didn't have. I don't know how I managed to drive, but I made it. I walked into the emergency waiting room. It was packed. I saw Hunter and we hugged like never before. I asked if he had been in to see his dad. He said he thought it was only right to wait till everyone was there.

I couldn't wait. I was directed to a little room where much of Daisy's family was gathered. My fears were confirmed. Rick had dived into the pool just like he had done three hours earlier in the day when he videotaped and posted it online. But this time he hit the top of his forehead on the bottom of the pool. He broke his neck, and was instantly dead. Daisy was the only one home at the time. She at first thought that he was messing around with her, as he floated on his belly. He always enjoyed playing tricks on her. Then she noticed bubbles coming out of his nose and mouth and rising past his ears. She freaked out and jumped in. He was unresponsive. She couldn't leave him to get to her phone to call 911.

She tried to do CPR in the water. Then she tried to get him out of the pool. She stuck his arms through the ladder on the side of the pool, and just kept shoving on him till she got him up on the deck. I don't know how she possibly could have done that by herself. He weighed at least 220 pounds. She got the EMTs out to the house and they worked on him for an hour. There just was nothing they could do.

The coroner asked me if I wanted to go back to see him. I have no words to describe what it felt like the first time I saw my son's dead body. I moved like a robot—somthing else was directing my moves. I couldn't function. He still had a blue endo-tracheal tube sticking out of his mouth about six inches. He was covered with a white sheet, and his head and upper extremities were visible. His hands. Oh my God his hands. So beautiful were his hands. So much like Pop's hands. He looked peacefully asleep. Except for that damn tube in his mouth.

Daisy was sobbing at his side, holding his hand, begging him to wake up. She needed him. He couldn't leave her. They had so many plans. Her life would be empty without him. She couldn't go on. Daisy's mom eventually said to Daisy that they should let me be alone with him. Daisy and I hugged. Her mom and I hugged. And we all cried.

I kissed his face, held his hand and whispered to him. I thanked him for getting back in my life. It had been wonderful to be with him those last three years. All the while as I sat next to his motionless body silent tears gently caressed my cheeks, and softly landed on his face, his hand, and the sheet that covered his body.

Joe arrived with Riley and Gunner. The two kids along with Hunter gathered up in a circle and hugged together. The crowd in the waiting area was filled with people who could do nothing but grieve for those kids who lost their mom seven years earlier. And now their dad lay dead in a small cold room deeper in the bowels of the hospital.

When the kids were ready, I walked them and Joe back to see their dad and son. I again held Rick's hand and kissed his forehead, mostly to help the kids know they could touch him, too. They stood motionless at his side, left to right, oldest to youngest. Tears were glistening on each of their grief-stricken faces. Yet they were mute. No sobbing. No yelling. No moving. Just ear-piercing silence. They looked to me like little kids again...like the ages they were when their mom died. None of them wanted to get close to his body. None of them wanted to touch him. Then, in a minute they were done, and seemed to glide out of that terrible space, like zombies. I followed them. The air itself felt like death.

The coroner stood by. She finally was able get my attention, and slowly, clearly stated that since the kids were not yet eighteen and Rick was not married, it would be up to Joe and me to make funeral arrangements. Oh, and by the way, would I want to donate any of his body parts? I wanted to donate as much as possible to help other people. And Joe and I agreed to make the funeral arrangements. My first thoughts were to take him back to Ohio and bury him next to my plot in the cemetery in Osgood. Joe had decided years before that he wanted to be cremated and have his ashes put out in a lake nearby. So that left me with an extra burial spot. My son would be next to me through all eternity. It seemed like a good idea at the time. It was a peaceful thought, all things considered.

Joe stayed alone with his son's body and begged him to squeeze his hand just once. Please Rick just squeeze his hand. He was so distraught. The sound of a man begging his dead son to come back to life is heart wrenching.

As we stood on the other side of the curtain from their dad's body, I asked the kids what they wanted done. Hunter didn't pause. Cremation. And put his ashes with Mom's. My god he seemed to have matured ten years in the short two years he had lived with his dad. He was their spokesman, the head of their shrinking family. His brother and sister agreed with him by nodding. No words spoken. Just whimpers. And tears drying on their cheeks as new tears escaped from their eyes.

There were still a lot of people in the waiting room when we went back out there. So many hugs and tears followed. It was clear that Rick was loved by many, many people in that small town. A lot of them introduced themselves and hugged me. I was so glad that he found his home with these people. Yet it was awful that his life ended so abruptly. Just when he was finding happiness. The whole thing was just unimaginable, surreal. People slowly filtered out of the waiting room.

I was the last one to leave the hospital parking lot. My phone rang. I was tempted to throw the damn thing out the window. How dare anyone call me in this time of turmoil. At ten o'clock at night. It was from the state donor network. I got part way through the verbal consent, and finally asked if we could continue this tomorrow. No way could I drive home all the while giving away my son's body parts. The drive home was indescribable. So many emotions. So much grief. What a jumbled up, empty, horrible mess.

And yet, there was the most extraordinary moon rise in the east that I have ever seen. The moon was huge, and the darkest orange color I've ever seen. There was a lot of dust in the air from farmers working the ground, so the edges of the moon appeared kind of foggy, like it was dissolving into the surrounding air. It felt like a sponge was soaking up my grief, and leaving my son's soft, strong presence in its place. As I kept glancing at it, I just knew I'd be able to get through what was to come. Whatever that might prove to be.

⚬ ⚬ ⚬ ⚬ ⚬

The next day, Wednesday, was a day of phone calls. Arranging the time to meet with Daisy and her mom at the funeral home, ended up being among the easiest of them. Talking to the state donor network was the most difficult. I was prepared for talking about harvesting things like his corneas. I hated hearing that word "harvesting" used in relation to cutting up my son's body. I was not prepared for talking about harvesting his heart valves, internal organs, skin, and long bones. For each part of Rick they wanted to harvest, I got an in-depth description of how the part would be removed, the care and respect it would receive, and how it would be used to improve the life of someone in need. The woman I talked to was very professional, and knowledgeable. It was sickening to hear a stranger talk so matter-of-factly about cutting up my son. I still felt raw from seeing Rick dead on that cold, hard table in the emergency room. But I knew somehow, that he would want this to be done.

I was about to scream at the woman as she described taking out the long bones. I interrupted her. They could have his bones—except for the bone in his right arm. My thinking was that the right side is exposed to mourners passing by the casket. If someone wanted to touch him, I wanted to know that they would be touching his arm, not some skin and muscle with a wooden dowel in the middle of it. She tried to argue about it, but I was done. My decision was made. His right upper arm bone stayed in his arm.

Joe and I drove up to the funeral home to make the arrangements. That was kind of odd, talking about our son who was now dead. It wasn't supposed to happen this way. We shouldn't outlive our kids. But never mind that. He was dead, and we were living. Daisy and her mom were already there. We were all very agreeable as we wrote the obituary and made the funeral plans.

Then on to the church we went. The viewing and funeral service would be in the main body of the church, followed immediately by the service. We agreed to three speakers, and I would give the main eulogy. The pastor was not all that convinced that I would be able to get through the eulogy and recommended I give him a copy before the service, and if necessary, he'd finish my words. I wasn't worried about a thing. I knew I would get through the day. But I ended up giving him a copy just to appease him.

In the meantime, I tried to let grow deep in my soul the writings of Kahlil Gibran in *The Prophet* (Alfred A. Knopf: New York, 1923.), a book I got from someone I dated way back in high school. I've read it dozens of times. There's a chapter titled "On Children" where Gibran suggests our children are not ours, but rather are the sons and daughters of Life. He goes on to suggest that we, as parents, are bows in an archer's hand—and I believe that the archer is God. It is God who releases the arrows (our children) from the bow (us as parents). And in that sense, it's possible for me to accept that my children belong to Life, to the archer, to God. I do not own them. I need to let them make their own way in their own lives. And let go when the time comes. So, I knew I could get through the eulogy. Rick had passed into the infinite. And his light shined bright in my soul.

I always interpreted "Life" and "the archer" in this passage to mean God. And in that sense, it's possible for me to accept that my children belong to Life, to the archer, to God. I do not own them. I need to let them make their own way in their own lives. And let go when the time comes. So, I knew I could get through the eulogy. Rick had passed into the infinite. And his light shined bright in my soul.

The next few days, my mind seemed to be acutely clear. So much to think about. So much to do. So much to grieve. I wanted Sophie and Josh to come to my house, so we could share some memories together and just talk. I wanted to grieve with them. Sophie and Jess came, but not Josh.

Since it didn't work out for Josh to come over, I decided to have some of my closest friends come over and visit in my backyard that Friday evening. It was so nice to have people close. We listened to music and talked about a lot of stuff. Towards the end of the evening we tried to put together the garden bench I had gotten from my brothers and sisters. It's a tradition in my family that the grieving sibling gets some special memorabilia from the rest of us when there's a death in the family. It was already dark out, and I didn't have enough flashlights to keep track of all the pieces once we tore into the box. So that didn't work out very well. But it sure was funny. I think we had the arm rests on backwards which would make it real interesting to sit down on it. Man, there were a lot of nuts and bolts in the box. Way more than we needed, it seemed like. The next morning it took me less than ten minutes to get it put together correctly. With all the right parts in all the right places.

CHAPTER 13

Now Comes the Funeral

I got to the church where the viewing and funeral were to take place plenty early. Daisy and her clan were already there. We had to wait to get into the sanctuary. Finally, the doors opened. We went in. There he lay. My God. He was beautiful. He looked like a movie star. The funeral director instructed me to not touch his face too much—it had taken a lot of makeup to hide the vast bruising. Joe and I each got a stool to sit on at the head of the casket. Daisy declined one. She stood on the other side of Joe from me.

People started filing in. I knew so many of Rick's friends. Some of my friends were able to make the trip there. All my brothers and sisters filed through and offered me their "deepest sympathy". That's what we were all taught to say at viewings. Sometimes in the past when I said the phrase to grieving people I thought the sentiment was a bit empty. But not that day. People who said it looked in my eyes with so much compassion. It was the perfect thing to say to me that day. I was amazed at the number of my family members and friends who were able to share that sacred day with me.

I noticed that people were trying to figure out where to sit. I asked the funeral director to save the left side for my family. Rick's friend Lois had already sat on the right side so Rick's friends could sit there. He put signs out that said "Reserved for Family" on the seats on the left side of the aisle. I meant the signs to indicate my family would be able to have seats there. But Daisy's family sat their butts right on in there. It was aggravating. As far as I was concerned, they were not family. They were friends. Rick did

121

not marry Daisy. They should be on the other side of the aisle. The service was about to start. I went to the back of church and got all my grandkids who were still sitting in the back of the church and made room for them close to me.

Several of the folks who knew Rick well—the people who got him off drugs, into the church, and got him work when he needed it said some words. Then it was my turn. I talked about some of the silly things that Rick had done as a kid, some of the struggles and challenges he overcame, the love he had for his children, and how happy he was to have found someone to marry again. There was laughter, followed by open sobbing at different times as I spoke. Some folks got emotional when I mentioned that his available organs were donated, and his corneas were already helping someone else see. I added that I imagined that people who got some of his body parts, would find themselves suddenly with a weird sense of humor and new joy of living, and then wonder why.

When I finished, I folded the paper I had written the eulogy on and gently slipped it into Rick's shirt pocket. Then I kissed his forehead and said good-by. Finally, I picked out a rose from the vase I had arranged to be by the casket, along with a locket of Rick's hair that the donor agency had sent me, and gave it to Joe, saying I was happy to have gotten Rick back again for these past three years. We hugged in that special way that only parents can do.

I gave a rose to Josh and Sophie and told them that he really did love them, though he didn't seem to show it very well at times when they were kids, and even as an adult. I gave a rose and locket of hair to Hunter, Riley, and Gunner and said he loved them more than anything in the whole world. I gently placed Katie's rose across Rick's chest and put his hand on top of the stem as I said to him how sad I was that he was somewhere else.

I gave a rose to each of Daisy's kids. Then a rose and locket of hair to Daisy. She and I held onto each other ever so tightly for several minutes. Her sobbing, and loud guttural shrieks of grief reverberated, and echoed through the sanctuary. Frankly, I was a little taken aback by her display, but I knew she had to let it rip, so we held on to each other, until she could release her grip on me and I could move enough to sit down.

The pastor talked for a little bit and then the crowd was instructed to leave the church through the back door. It seemed to take an eternity for people to start to leave. I was about to look back to see what the holdup was. Then my sister, Ginger, finally came up to the front. She stopped by the casket. Then walked on. What a relief—people were finally getting out. I felt a hand on my shoulder, and looked up to see my cousin, Julie. She had lost her husband three years before. We hugged. And cried. And understood grief together.

Then there was a long line of people loving on me again. One of Rick's friends, I think it was Clarise, was so moved by the part of the eulogy about the organ donation that she said was going to donate her organs as well. She planned to sign the paperwork the next week. Most everybody else just held my hands and looked into my eyes with tears in theirs. For them there were no words to be said.

To three of my brothers I whispered, "I hope I get to be as full of shit as you!" as I hugged them. I was so relieved to hear some laughter from each of them. Marky came up to me, held my hand, hugged me and said nothing. The pain he felt for me seared through his teary eyes into mine. His silence gave me strength. Hank shook my hand, and voiced sorrow again. He was quiet, no real emotion. Mariam had no words. We shared our grief as she hugged me. Helen's hug included her statement, "I could not have done what you just did."

The funeral director came up to me and said, "Those three people back there won't leave." I looked in the direction he pointed. Some of my best friends in the world, Sally, her man, and Traci Jo, wouldn't leave me. My heart soared. I told him they could stay as long as they wanted. The next time I looked back there, they were gone. I kind of wished they were still there when I noticed their absence. It felt good to think someone was watching over me. It was somehow very comforting.

When all the people were out except immediate family, Joe, Daisy and I were asked to stand near the casket and pull the veil up over Rick's face. I had a nagging feeling that it should be his kids doing this. Not us three. I said nothing. But I still wish I would have taken his kids up there for them to have a last moment with him. I wish they would have been able to cover him one last time. Just as he had covered them and protected them as best he could when they were babies. Yet there the three of us stood. Each of us with a hand on the veil. Rick's life flashed before me. How he changed my sense of self when he was a baby. All the love he brought to our family as a kid. All the confusion and despair I felt as drugs took him away from me. All the delight and pride his kids bring us. The ecstasy of getting him back in my life once he conquered his addiction. And finally, the shock of losing him to death. How could I survive this?

We escorted Rick's body out of church and onto the hearse. It still brings a tear to my eye now as I think about the hearse carrying my son's body away from me for the very last time. It would soon be turned to ashes. All the joy and love and heartache that boy brought into my life rounded the corner of the church and disappeared. Snap! Just like that.

Then we went inside for the best funeral lunch ever. Barbeque ribs, with all the fixins'. It would have been their wedding dinner menu. Rick had made the down payment on the food already. One of Rick's friends made the arrangements for a local restaurant to cook the meal. I really appreciated that.

I sat at the table with Rick's three kids to eat. It was hard to swallow the delicious food. I asked them if they wanted any of their dad's ashes. Gunner asked, "Why? I already got his hair!" I love that kid. Hunter thought all the ashes should be kept together and placed with all of Mom's. Riley said she wanted some; she wanted to make them into jewelry, and some day clone him. Right.

Before I left, I noticed that someone from church gave a DVD to Daisy. I had requested and paid for a video of the service and wondered what they gave her. I never did get the video. We divided up the flowers and left. Another long ride home.

Alone with my memories and my sorrow.

Author's home place as a child.

Author at five years old, Christmas morning.

Author's high school
graduation picture.

Joe's high school graduation picture.

Strohs sisters
Top row: Esther, Author, Lenore.
Bottom row: Mary, Aggie, Sally.

Rick and Josh in Texas.

Young Rick, Josh, Sophie.

Sophie, Rick and Josh on the first day of Rick's senior year.

Katie in my back yard, the last day I saw her.

Riley, Hunter, Rick, Gunner at Riverscape
the first time they were together in 6 years.

Rick with German beer stein.

CHAPTER 14

Gloom Despair and Agony on Me

Whew, boy howdy, things took a turn for the worst in the weeks following the funeral. I had to go to talk to the lawyer out there every week for about two months. I wasn't executor of his estate because he didn't own enough for it to be considered an estate. As his mother I was his next of kin. So, it was up to me to get his bills paid and make things right in the eyes of the law.

Hunter had no place to live, really, so I helped him out as much as I could as he continued to work at the lumber company. He didn't feel comfortable being at Daisy's even before Rick died. They had made up a bedroom for him but it just wasn't home to him.

Lois, whom I thought of as a dear friend, called me just about everything but a white woman in her long texts. She accused me of freezing Rick's bank accounts, so she couldn't pay his workers. Of course, I didn't do that. Bank accounts are frozen the day a person dies.

She told me I was a mean old drunk, and Rick hated me. And he always did. According to her, she and Rick apparently decided that she was more of a mom to him than I ever was. She started to treat Hunter like crap. She accused him of using drugs, even being a dealer, and stealing things from Daisy. She put the family pictures and other memorabilia of Rick's she had collected from Daisy out in the rain. It was all pretty much destroyed. Her family seemed to go out of their way to harass Hunter. I finally just responded with "Do not contact me or my grandkids again" every time she texted. This was a woman who was dear to my son.

And I also thought the world of her. I loved her for saving Rick from drugs and being his friend. And I probably always will. Why she treated me like that goes beyond any understanding. Maybe it was just her way of grieving the loss of someone she dearly loved.

I didn't hear one peep from Daisy as other people claimed to be her spokespersons. Daisy did meet with the lawyer and said in no uncertain terms that she felt she should be allowed to keep everything that was Rick's. Everything he got during the time they were together. Even everything he had before that. What? Everything? Rick had probably at least $20,000 of automotive tools. He had gotten many of them for his boys. What was she going to do with all of them? Of course, other friends claimed the tools were theirs. Unbelievable. But okay. There was nothing legally I could do to get anything from her unless I wanted to pay a lawyer more than all of it was worth.

Hunter wanted small things like the wooden spoon that hung in the kitchen above the stove at Rick's house. It had been Mom's and he remembered it from times when he was a little kid. He wanted his mom and dad's Bible, and tools that he and Rick had bought together. If he could have gotten just what he thought was his, he would have a good start. Well at least a better start. He'd be able to fix stuff. They claimed that all he was entitled to was an air compressor that didn't work. What a strang thing to do, I thought.

Even Gunner finally acknowledged that he thought he and Hunter should have what their dad bought for them. He described times he went shopping with Rick and Rick got several hundreds of dollars worth of tools he wanted Gunner to have. It was heartbreaking to hear the boys ask me over and over to help them get back what they thought was rightly theirs. Till they finally accepted they got nothing of their dad's.

There were some things I wanted back that I had given Rick: a beer stein from Germany, and a lap blanket that Pop used in the nursing home and probably died under. I gave the blanket to Rick that first winter we were reconnected. He told me he stayed warm under it in his car at night when he was piloting, so he wouldn't have to spend money on a hotel room. I'd still like to have it back. Yet I know I'll never see either of those things again.

Daisy knew Rick for two years. I knew him his whole life. And Hunter, Riley, and Gunner were alive because of him. It just didn't make a lick of sense. The whole thing got downright ugly, hateful and very painful.

Finally, six weeks after the funeral, I got the call from the funeral director that Rick's ashes were released by the coroner. I texted Daisy and asked if she wanted me to drop off her "share" of ashes at her house. She was working that day and wouldn't be home when I planned to stop by her place. So, I went about my business with the lawyer, visited with Hunter and eventually went to the funeral home to get Rick's ashes. I didn't want to do it, but I asked them to separate the ashes into one-fourth and three-fourths. The funeral director asked if he could carry my son out to the car for me. He did so with much loving concern.

I faced another long drive home. Alone. With my dead son's ashes in the back seat.

I could see the Dayton skyline, when I got a text from Daisy. Would I like to stop by for a sandwich? I texted back that I was almost home. And so, I declined the visit and let her know I'd drive out there again over the upcoming weekend.

Before I drove the last six miles home, all hell broke loose. Daisy's mom texted me—"Why are you keeping Rick's ashes from Daisy?" I had no intention of keeping his ashes. I don't like the whole idea of cremation. I didn't want his ashes. I wanted him to be alive. But I couldn't have that. So, I wanted his body to be whole and resting next to mine in my hometown cemetery plot for all eternity. I couldn't have that either. He was dust in the wind.

I have felt at a loss over a lot of things in my life, but this really hurt. I got advice from so many people over the next few weeks. I was told I needed to give her the ashes. Hunter adamantly insisted that all his Dad's ashes should be with all of his Mom's ashes.

I determined that I would not give Daisy any of the ashes until his three kids agreed to the same plan. I was getting it from all sides. Not many people agreed with Hunter, but I would not share Rick's ashes until his kids agreed that's what they all wanted to do. His kids are more important to me than all those other people ever were, or ever could be.

Dammit I really regretted allowing the funeral to be so much about Daisy and her family, rather than my family and especially Rick's kids. I will never forgive myself for that. Never.

Todd, Rick's friend since junior high ended up homeless after Rick was gone. Eventually he drifted back to Dayton and was staying with his cousins. He called me every now and then to borrow some money to buy gas, so he could get to a job he had. Or so he said. He informed me that he was a bouncer at some bar. It was kind of hard for me to believe that a bar would hire a man to work as a bouncer who had only one leg to stand on. But I accepted his story. And didn't give him any money. Next thing I heard about him, was that he got beat up trying to overtake someone who didn't feel a need to pay his bar bill before he left the establishment. And then Todd moved in with Joe, Riley and Gunner. Hunter was still in Happy Hills.

I thought that Todd living with Joe and the kids was not such a good idea. Riley had just gotten out of a residential treatment center, seemed to be struggling with some social issues, and was still adjusting to having so much more freedom at Joe's. The first time Riley got in trouble with the law, was when she got pulled over, and Todd slipped some of his drug paraphernalia under her seat. She didn't even know about the drugs he had. She was charged with possession. Todd was not charged with anything. I was furious.

Todd wrecked Joe's van two or three times, and finally Joe had enough. He dropped Todd off at his Mom's about forty miles from town. Hunter was quiet about what he knew about Todd until he was out of the house; there was a $10,000 reward on Todd's head in Kentucky for traffic citations and drug violations. Hunter said he wouldn't turn him in because that's not what a friend would do. And Todd was Hunter's dad's best friend, after all.

Todd died of a drug over dose a few weeks later. I feel empty thinking about his life.

So, I waited and grieved. Many times, over the summer I sat on the garden bench that my family gave me and tried to figure things out. I looked through the same space, breathed the same air, and smelled the same scents as I did before when I was in my backyard. And yet nothing was the same. Nothing was the way I wanted it to be. I got lots of support from some of my family and friends through this long, hot summer. And I spent a lot of time alone. Sad and alone.

When fall rolled around, the love and support I felt from so many people shortly after Rick's death seemed to dry up. It just seemed like folks didn't have time to do stuff with me. What happened to all the people who said they'd always be there for me? But after giving it some more thought, I concluded that it's common for survivors to be left alone several weeks after the funeral. I've heard that a lot of people try to figure out how long they think someone should grieve for a family member who died which is generally about six to eight weeks. Then if the family seems to be doing okay they figure the family is "over it", and have accepted the new normal. I get that. And mostly I was doing well. I was getting out and about. I went back to work and started playing golf the week after Rick's funeral. At a minimum I was going through the motions of living. Inside, I was hurting.

It was tough going. I just felt overwhelmingly sad and I wanted to be around people doing fun stuff. I wanted things to be like the summer before. And all the summers before that when I was so busy with friends, and work, and travel. Yet my state of mind wouldn't let me do fun stuff. So, instead I sat home alone night after night. I felt somehow paralyzed, or something. Sometimes I would call people, but generally they were busy. I tried to reach out to Sally. She was always my go-to friend. But she was doing a lot with her yard and trees and didn't want to leave the house. Or she had plans for things with other friends. I totally understood; she had other things to do. Can't hold that against her. Strohs Sister Esther was easy to talk to. We still connected intermittently on a deep emotional level. She helped me a lot. My sister Ginger called to check on me regularly, and mostly I just wasn't up to going anywhere or doing anything. Even with her. She had been my rock my whole life. And now things were different. I can't explain it. Even my sister, Frances in Alaska called regularly too. I know she was worried about me, but there were no words to put to my grief that she or anyone could understand. Or do anything about.

I continued to prod Hunter to decide about his dad's ashes. I was getting to the point that I just couldn't let this go unresolved through Rick's upcoming birthday in the fall. Finally, Hunter said, "Okay I'll get my head out of my ass. We can give Daisy some of Dad's ashes." It just makes me sick to think about this, all this time later. Hunter wanted all his dad to be with all his mom's ashes. Period. I think that no one outside of our family had a right to voice an opinion to me on this subject. This very personal, sorrowful issue still leaves me feeling beat up and bruised.

The day before Thanksgiving six months after Rick died, what was left of our family met at the cemetery where Ashley's ashes are. It was cold and windy. Riley and Joe came shortly after I arrived. Joe was quiet, pensive. Riley didn't really seem to be at all present mentally. Her eyes were red and swollen.

Once everyone else got there, we started. I opened with a prayer and said a few words. Joe said a few words. Josh stood there with tears welling up in his eyes. He had no words to say. Nothing came out of his mouth. Sophie said she wasn't going to lie. Rick had treated her awful when they were kids. Some of the things he did were just plain unforgivable. But she really wished she had tried to get to know him these last three years when she had the opportunity. It was clear he had changed. Now she would never know what kind of man he turned into. She wished she had given him a chance to prove himself to her. She wished she could have loved him.

By this time, Riley was in the car inconsolable and probably craving something that would make her feel better and cover up the pain. Hunter said simply, he didn't know who he would be if he hadn't moved in with his dad two years before. His voice trailed off into quiet tears. Gunner had nothing to say. He seemed a bit mixed up about what he was feeling, and what to do. We all held hands and prayed. Then we went out to dinner.

As we sat at the table, I couldn't help but think that my family had experienced enough pain and heartache. And deep down inside, I also knew I would never have the family connectedness, and love within my family that I always expected and hoped for when I was growing up on the farm. My family was shattered and scarred. I will never sit with all my kids and grandkids for dinner. I will never feel that joy, and pride, and happiness. My future looked empty and sad and lonely and bleak.

Hunter and I made one last trip to Dry Gulch two days later. It was the day after Thanksgiving. He had to pick up some tires from his friend. And we dropped off some of Rick's ashes to Daisy. I backed the whole way up the half-mile driveway. The same driveway I had loved driving down earlier that year to spend time with my son. Now it just felt sad. I didn't want to be there.

Hunter got out of my truck and went in the house. A short time later he came back out. Daisy didn't come out to talk to me. Of course, I didn't make any effort to go inside either. I just couldn't. Hunter was inside for a little while, then came out and went around to the back of the house. He picked up a box of stuff from the back porch and away we went. In the box was what Daisy claimed was Ashley's bible. Hunter said it was a lot smaller than he remembered. I knew it wasn't her bible. I had given her the bible for a wedding gift, but I kept that bit of information to myself. Another thing in the box was the maroon velvet bag with the gold sash that had cradled Ashley's ashes all those years ago. How that survived to get to Hunter that day still baffles the mind. It was a long, quiet, confusing ride home. There still seemed to be so many unanswered questions. So many loose ends were impossible to tie up.

The weekend after that, the fire department in the small town I grew up in conducted a training exercise for new firemen in the house that had been our family home since 1929. It was built in 1878 and had stood empty for decades. Wow, what an emotional thing that was to witness. A flood of memories raced through my mind as I watched windows explode from the heat of the fire inside the house, and flames rip through those gaping holes. I could picture Mom doing the dishes, making sure she wiped down each piece before any bubbles could dry on them as she stood and gazed out the kitchen window. What a great life she must have felt like she had. She had twelve children and sixty grandchildren. That should get her a spot in heaven right next to God himself. I could picture Pop sitting in his favorite rocking chair (the same one I now sit in at my house) reading the newspaper or holding the newest grandchild and letting them listen to his pocket watch which he called his "tick-tock." I recalled so many meals eaten, holidays celebrated, and babies held. Now the structure that held those memories was going up in flames. Sally took time to stop by and shed a tear with me. She had a plethora of fond memories in that house, too. We shared some of them. We always were and remain more like sisters than friends. What a day.

She left there and went to visit her mom for the last time. The day after that, Sally's mom died. Holy crap. Way too much stuff going on. I went to her mom's funeral. I didn't go to the lunch afterward. I just had too much turmoil swirling in my soul to be near people suffering a loss themselves. I couldn't do that then. Instead I went to my home place and loaded up some bricks that were left from the house I grew up in. They all laid in a burned-up heap. I, my brothers and sisters, and all my nieces and nephews grew up in that house. And I was collecting bricks to take home to remember them and this time of my life.

It was also Rick's fortieth birthday.

The house the author grew up in, providing a training
exercise for new firemen. Memories up in flames.

CHAPTER 15

Our New Norm

The Christmas holiday that year was way different from any in the past. I didn't want to have people over. I didn't want to celebrate anything. Life just seemed kind of empty. But we did get together. Not much joviality. Not much happiness. But those of us who were still living, tried to wrap our heads around our new reality.

Two days into the New Year, Riley was admitted to a hospital. She was acting unstable and appeared to have a lot of belly pain. But she was discharged home with pain meds once the pain was better controlled. Riley was admitted back to the hospital a few days later, with excruciating belly pain this time. The charge nurse identified her as a drug seeker and imitated her with flailing arms and legs and screams for meds to relieve the terrible pain. She and some of the other staff were laughing about it in the nurses' station, in full view of me and anyone else passing by. I didn't think it was funny. That was my granddaughter suffering and they were making fun of her. As it turns out Riley needed an appendectomy—it may have burst before she got into surgery, which would have been a life-threatening situation. Now that would hurt. Realizing this got me even more upset with the nursing staff there.

I went to visit her once she got home. Home at the time for her was a friend's apartment where she was staying while he was out of town. She still had drainage tubes in her belly which confirmed my belief that her pre-surgery condition was indeed very serious. She just absolutely could not get comfortable. She had taken all but three and a half of the pain pills she was given—narcotics of course—but should been have at least twenty left. I did my best to make her comfortable. Nothing helped.

Finally, she looked at me and said, "Screw it Grandma, just leave!"

That was the last time I saw her.

CHAPTER 16

Six Months Later

A few months later, in the spring 2017, I went to the cemetery to sit with Rick. It had been a year since his death. We talked. I asked him how he liked his neighbors. They seemed to all be quite a bit older than him, I noticed. He didn't answer. But I could almost hear him laugh.

Gunner had been going through a major transformation. And it was awesome. He was tall and slender and very strong. I didn't see that coming. He presents himself very well to adults and fits well into almost every situation. He can carry on an intelligent conversation with nearly anyone. He's smart, poised, and self-controlled. He still likes his four-wheelers and has some cool friends.

Memorial Day weekend, Hunter graduated from high school. Joe and I sat up in the top row at the Nutter Center where the graduation ceremony was held. He said he always hoped this day would come, but he wasn't always so sure it would happen. It was a very happy event. We were both proud and relieved that Hunter made it. He had grown and matured in amazing ways as well. He joined the Army National Guard. He's on his way to becoming a mechanic. He has a good group of friends, and a wonderful girlfriend. I enjoy every minute I spend with them. They make me laugh.

As I was driving home from the graduation ceremony, I got a call from Riley. She was stuck in Florida. She told me she had gotten arrested when her boyfriend was driving a stolen car—"but it wasn't really stolen." She and her boyfriend "just borrowed" it from his mom. Here we go again. Seems like misunderstandings get her in trouble a lot of times. She wants to come back to Ohio, yet she knows she will have to clear up several legal issues which could land her in prison. Talk about being stuck between a rock and a hard place!

She tried to explain things to me in the fifteen minutes we had available to talk. She said she doesn't miss drugs while she can't get them. I said maybe she should try to stay away from people who use drugs once she gets out of jail. She asked me if I had ever been an addict. I said I hadn't. She tried to explain that it's really, really hard to be an addict. There's so much to deal with. You know that if you continue using the drugs they will kill you. And yet you just can't stop the feeling that you need them. You feel dead inside, and yet you crave the very thing that is killing you. At one point she said that drug addicts really do care about their friends. Addicts are very loving and take in people who don't have a place to stay. The only problem is that they are not reliable. I laughed at that and she giggled, too. Then to top it off she identified some of her emotional issues. She seemed so all together all together that day. But she realized she still had a lot to contend with before she can really get on with her life. She realized she had messed things up bad. She wants to come home and be around family.

I know Riley is going to make it. She's on the right track. She's going to be okay. She will make things right and come back home. She said she wants to write a book about her life because she's never met anyone who has the same multi-faceted problems. I can't imagine the horror she must feel during the normal course of her day.

But that's another story. A story I hope to help her write. Soon.

Safe Harbor

The first several years after Katie was adopted, we continued to get pictures, and stories about her. She was the princess of the neighborhood in her new town. She loved Dora the Explorer and that was the theme of her bedroom. She was happy. You could see it in her eyes and her smile. We haven't heard from the aunt we know in the past few years. She seemed to get a bit uncomfortable when I'd stop by her office. Also, I trust these folks to take care of Katie. And they deserve their privacy. That's the way they wanted it when they took my baby girl into their family.

Jess saw Katie and her new grandma recently at the grocery store nearby. They didn't talk. Katie didn't see the aunt who kept her safe for three years. It's just so weird.

I still believe that letting her be adopted into such a loving, caring family was the right thing to do. It's weird to acknowledge that some other people are raising her as their own. Sometimes it's hard to accept God's plan. This one never has and never will make sense. But I guess I don't need to understand why this happened to know that she's right where she needs to be. God gave us His son. We gave that family our Katie. It was the only thing to do.

I had learned she was living in a suburb of Cleveland. Before I started writing this book, I drove out to the suburb and imagined I was seeing things she could see. I knew she was baptized in the Catholic Church—which makes me even more positive that she belongs with this family. I found a church called Our Lady of Perpetual Help. That certainly seemed apropos for the situation. I went in. I breathed air that I hoped Katie and her family had breathed. I sat in a pew for a long time.

I kind of hoped she would walk in and I would recognize her. That would be so exciting. We could restart a life together. I wanted to hear about her parents, brothers, friends, and all the stuff she likes to do. I wanted to throw a softball to her. Then I was scared she would walk in and I would recognize her and want to hug her. And I wouldn't know what to do and her mom would be pissed at me for interfering with their lives. I left the church and drove around till I found a sports park. Hoover Park. Soccer fields, ball diamonds. I hoped I was seeing places Katie would maybe be going to while she's growing up.

Katie. She's the first person I think of in the morning and the last person I think of before I go to sleep. Every day I thank her new parents through my prayers for giving Katie such a great life. A much better life than we could have given her with all the craziness that goes on in our family. That's a tough thing to admit, and no one in my immediate family would dispute it.

Several times a year, I write her a letter, or get her a card. I put $20 plus a dollar for every year she's lived in her birthday card just like I do for the other grandkids. I get Christmas cards, and Valentine's Day cards and write notes to her. I have all of them in her Christmas stocking. It's getting thick! I hope I get to see her and get to know her and love her in person. I want to be her Grumma again.

Katie
Always loved
never forgotten

Rick's Eulogy

I've often said to people in their time of grief and sorrow that it's OK to cry. In fact, the more you cry, the less you have to pee. Well today's the day to let the tears flow with reckless abandon.

Rick was born in Wilford Hall Air Force Hospital, in San Antonio, Texas. Coming from a state that seemingly has no bounds, apparently got him started on his path in life. He seemed to have no boundaries either. Not in fun. Not in love. Not in living.

I compiled some memories some are just random thoughts, some short stories—of the life he had before finding his home in Happy Hills.

Rick loved his little brother and sister Josh and Sophie. Most of the time he was a bit mysterious about how he showed his love. And it might not have felt like love at all sometimes. One of his favorite pastimes was teasing them and he was good at that. Sometimes it went beyond teasing like dropping a couch on Josh's head or telling Sophie to store her bike in the place where they put dead people at the park storm drains. His adventuresome nature lead to doing dumb stuff. He'd do almost anything—if it was dangerous enough. Josh told me last week, "Every single time Rick put my life in danger, he made sure to go out of his way to save it!" True love there! To drive Sophie nuts he would say "I always do what Sophie says."

His favorite breakfast was Ricky eggs scrambled eggs, with cheese and sliced hot dogs.

He showed Josh and Sophie how to do stuff. In no time at all our front yard had hardly any grass because of their superior ability to tear it up with their big wheels. Big wheels turned into bicycles, and he was able to go many miles in one day not just our yard. He loved to play softball and one year he got a traveling team together in just a few hours. He was a maniac on the ski slopes and sledding hills. Not sure how he survived some of that stuff.

Joe and I were dumb enough to get the kids a trampoline—only to find them jumping from the house roof on to it.

Sometimes he would take a notion to jump into water from high places like railroad trellises or the Huffman Dam. How ironic that the simple act of jumping in the pool in his back yard would be the thing that would end his life.

When Rick decided to do something, he would stick to it. In about the 4th grade he decided to stop eating anything green. I don't know why he chose to do that. As far as I know he never ate green again did.

On Halloween one year the 2 boys decided to do something scary when people came trick or treating. It just happened to be on a day that year that I was with my mom, so I wasn't there to stop it. Josh and Rick each dressed up like Zombies. Rick hooked up a block and tackle with a rope in one of our big maple trees out front. Josh poised himself in the tree, and Rick sat motionless on the front porch. At just the right time when some unsuspecting innocent little kids would walk up, Rick would loosen up on the rope, and Josh would seem to fall out of the tree. One time, the rope got away from Rick a bit too much, and Josh's nose actually touched the sidewalk just as Rick regained control of the rope. I was aghast when I heard what they did. They figured everything was OK they had taken the safety precaution of putting a pillow up Josh's shirt. They must have really scared some little kids because as I recall now, we didn't have many trick-or-treaters after that.

Maybe that stunt was partial payback to me for when Rick was younger, and he was in the bathroom I got real close to the window right next to his head and yelled BOO! He looked at the floor behind him, looked at me at said MOM. I could hardly stop laughing long enough to apologize and tell him I'd clean it up. It was then that I realized I really can scare the crap out of someone.

Rick had loads of first cousins. Ginger's kids lived closest to us, and they played together a lot. One day they tried the purse game down the street from our house. They attached a string to a purse, put it in the middle of the road, and then hid. When someone would try to get it, they would pull the string a little bit and freak the person out. They came back home after a while with their shoulders slumped, and their tails between their legs. His cousin said, "People in this town have no sense of humor." I never did find out what really happened. Probably best.

Rick and Josh's first car was a Dodge Aires which they dug out of the snow in grandma and grandpa Wellkamp's back yard. It worked pretty good once they got the pop cycle sticks, and vice grips attached at the right places with duct tape. You had to get under the hood to change gears. It might be true what they told me—that if you could floor it going down hill with a good tail wind, you might be able to get it up to 60 after about a mile. All I know is they never got a speeding ticket.

Then there's the story of Rick 'borrowing' some farmer's horse and riding it through the Taco Bell drive through—no saddle no bridle.

Rick had the good fortune to work at my cousin's for several years as they cleared land and built a log home. My cousin said that many times Rick watched him struggle to fix something, and after a while Rick would say, "Why don't you do it this way?" He was always right. It was always easier his way.

Rick married a girl from his hometown, Ashley. They were young and poor. Sometimes they didn't have two nickels nickels to rub together, but boy did they love their kids. Life was tough for them as they traveled from job to job, town to town. And then Ashley died in an accident. The twins were ten Gunner was five. I can't imagine what it's like for you to *now* lose your dad too. Maybe some day you'll understand that they really did love you.

I lost track of Rick for about six years. During that time there was a fog over my heart, not knowing where he was, or *if* he was. He contacted Joe three years ago—shortly after his own near death experience. We met, he reconnected with his kids, and I started to get to know him all over again. I am so grateful to have had this time with him, short as it was. We came to understand and love each other very deeply. And wow did his kids get to have good times with him dirt bikes, four wheelers, lots of laughs.

Rick fell in love with the best possible person for him, Daisy. You are the love of his life. I can't express how happy it makes me to know you found each other. Last Tuesday I'm absolutely certain sure when he woke up he was the happiest man on earth. Because of you and this whole great big Happy Hills family he found home for the first time. And I thank you all for keeping him safe for us these last years.

Rick and Daisy bought a place out in the country this past March. And were planning to get married in the barn on July 23. I came up to work on the place several times. One time, Daisy was trying to get him to do something, she got aggravated and walked away. Rick looked at me grinning and said 'I love that woman". Later we were standing in the barn yard, Daisy asked, "Nancy do you think we should have an outhouse?" I said—well I don't know. My brother Vernon missed his after he took it down". Rick said, "What if I can make it flush?" I said "How are you going to get an outhouse to flush?! He just laughed and said, "I didn't figure that out yet." I'll bet he would have—given more time.

He asked me a couple weeks ago if I remembered what I said the first time I saw where he lived in Happy Hills. I didn't. He reminded me that I said, "I never pictured you living here". It was the basement of an old funeral home converted into apartments. At the time we were talking about this, we were standing in the back yard of his new home out in the country. I looked around and said, "This is where I pictured you living till the end of your time".

We both smiled and took in the moment. Not knowing how soon the end of time would come for him.

The quote on my church envelope last Sunday was "You are intelligent and talented, but it seems to have escaped your mind that all these gifts and abilities are on loan to you. Be mindful. You are a temporary steward of these things, and you will be called upon to one day to give an account of how you used them."

Following that, I felt it only right to have as much of Rick's body 'harvested' so others can have a better life. This will help possibly as many as 300 people. His corneas have already helped two people see. I hope that every person that gets a piece of him will be just a little more adventuresome and silly. And wonder why.

From all the people who came before us, through all the people who live here now, to all the people who are to follow us, may we all be joined together; and love each other, as our heavenly father intended it to be. AMEN?

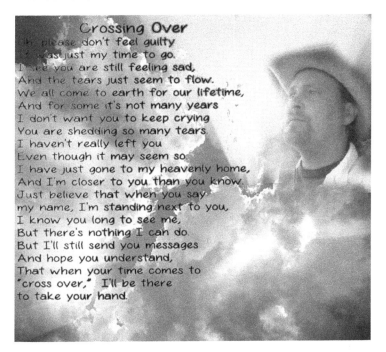

Crossing Over

In please don't feel guilty
as just my time to go.
I see you are still feeling sad,
And the tears just seem to flow.
We all come to earth for our lifetime,
And for some it's not many years
I don't want you to keep crying
You are shedding so many tears.
I haven't really left you
Even though it may seem so.
I have just gone to my heavenly home,
And I'm closer to you than you know.
Just believe that when you say
my name, I'm standing next to you,
I know you long to see me,
But there's nothing I can do.
But I'll still send you messages
And hope you understand,
That when your time comes to
"cross over," I'll be there
to take your hand.

Afterthoughts

As I said in the beginning of this book, it's been an interesting ride as a mother these last forty years. Throughout Rick's early adult years, I tried to figure out what I did that was so wrong, to raise a son who ended up such a mess. All the ridiculous things he did. All the risk taking. All the drug use. Not being able to keep a job or take care of his kids. I figured it must certainly be my fault. Maybe if I had done this or that differently he wouldn't have turned out the way he did.

Joe and I drove ourselves crazy trying to figure out just what we could have done to have avoided all the pain and turmoil in our family. Rick went to church with us every Sunday for as long as he lived with us, and we prayed the rosary and read the bible together in the evening, so lack of faith or teaching wouldn't be it. Joe and I each had college degrees, good jobs and were very involved with our church and the kids' activities—so it wouldn't be lack of family support, security, or food. We tried to keep him connected to our extended families and he seemed to enjoy being with cousins, uncles, aunts, and grandparents on my side as well as Joe's side of the family. And ironically, he went to both Joe's and my family Christmas parties six months before he died. It was the first time since high school that he went to any of the family parties.

I try to live with no regrets. I try to believe that I really didn't do all that much stuff wrong. That Rick was just Rick and he made decisions based on his internal circuits. And like Sophie used to say, I couldn't change him into something he wasn't. No matter what I did. Still it sucks the way things turned out. And I wish he was still alive.

Some people seem to think that losing an adult child can't be as bad as losing a young child. Some people seem to think it's been a long enough grief time for me, and I shouldn't need to talk about him anymore. Some people don't have a clue as to how hard it is to carry on a conversation with them about my life when they have spouses and children who are healthy and successful, while I have just a cat to welcome me home. I admit that if someone told me my story for the first time, I would have a hard time responding to it, too. I'd probably be speechless. Some people seem to think that losing Rick probably isn't so bad—I still have two other kids alive. I feel stabbed in the front, when I hear that. My other two kids can never fill the void that is left where Rick's joy, and love—his very soul—used to reside in my heart.

I checked with my sister-in-law about some of these questions. One of her eighteen children died as a young adult thirty some years ago. She said, "You think about them in the morning when you get up until the night time when you go to sleep. You never stop missing them." I agree wholeheartedly.

Some people ask me why on earth I would write a book about the horrible things that crept into my life. They say writing a book will just cut open the scars and make things worse. I do have to admit that I am amazed at how the memories again flooded out and were crystal clear as the words describing them landed on my computer screen. It was like I was reliving the scenes of my past life in real time. It was painful to write this book. And it has been a release. In the six months following Rick's death, I participated in several seminars related to drug abuse. It was awful dragging myself through all that mess again. I didn't want to be known by strangers as the mother of a drug addict. And yet, for some reason, I felt compelled to do it.

Last fall I felt so deserted, and alone. Somehow through that lonely time I knew I had to write this book. I realized my life was taking yet another turn. During that time, I came to know at a very deep level, that the ferocious demons of addiction took swatches of my life away when they took control of my son, and daughter-in-law. And even though he got back control of his life when he overcame his addictions, and he proved to be an amazing adult, his death leaves an empty space where his life should be, and a fractured family that may never heal. And some kids who are growing into adulthood, without him.

I realized then, last fall, that I was called upon to tell my story. I really don't have a choice. To not do this would be to turn away from my given purpose in life whatever that might prove to be when the last chapter of my life has been written. Hopefully, it will help others understand some of the things families of drug addicts go through. How drug addiction can happen in just about any family, to just about any person. And how it impacts generations of their family.

I'm beginning to believe that once a person is addicted to drugs or alcohol, they somehow know that what they do is wrong and stupid. But they don't know how to stop, nor can they figure out why they need to have it. They spend their money on drugs and alcohol because they can't live without it; to the point of losing their spouse, their family, their job, their home. They still love their family and friends in much the same way as they always did. And I think they don't understand why people perceive them differently, and don't want them around. It seems like they live in a fog of some kind of alternate reality. Like everybody else is wrong and they are living right. Take it or leave it.

One of my hesitations about writing this book, is I fear how the story based in part on my life experiences will be viewed. Will I be judged as a terrible person? Will people ask me why didn't I do something this way or that way? How could I be so stupid? How could I not figure out that something was horribly wrong? So that's something I'll have to deal with as the future unfolds in this new realm of my life. I do hope that folks who read it will be able to accept that I did the best I knew how. I have felt abandoned, and hated, and disrespected on so many levels in the past four decades. Now I hope that when my days are nearing the end, I can look back on them and think, "I laughed more than I cried."

I'll have to live a long time before I can honestly say that.

I do now somehow feel a deep, genuine, happiness and joy in my heart and soul. I don't know where it comes from. At times I don't understand how I can feel happiness or joy on any level. But it's there and I'm grateful for it. I still feel the same way inside that I felt when I was a little girl growing up on the farm, and I was so content. So full of life. So ready to heed Pop's directive: "Do mus spas haben!"

I'm trying, Pop! I'm really trying.

Book Club/Study Guide Questions

1. Introduction. What are your thoughts on the reasons for the high levels of excessive drug use today? Is it more related to the parents, economic status, lack of church involvement? What?

2. Katie Part 1: Unsafe harbor. What was going through your mind as you read about the terrible things Katie experienced as a fetus related to her mother using drugs while she was pregnant? How did you feel when you realized Katie is my granddaughter? What would you have done?

3. Chapter 1: My Early Life. If you're from a small family, could you imagine all those people eating together at the supper table? If you're an older adult from a large family, were you drawn back to memories of your own childhood? Did you find it gross when I wrote about mice trying to find an escape route from the stomachs of my dog and cat, or butchering chickens and rabbits? What kinds of things did you do for fun in high school? Do you remember your first kiss, make-out session? Did you ever have a hickey? Did you feel similar things about a strong desire to get away from home when you were out of high school? Were you encouraged to go to college? Do you think I married too young?

4. Chapter 3: My Early Motherhood. How did you feel when you were expecting your first baby? Were you confident as a new parent? Did you have help from family, friends when your kids were young? Did your kids have jobs at a young age?

5. Chapter 4: Rick's Teenage Years. How did your kids get along when they were in high school? Did you know of the times they got into trouble? If you were a counselor, would you be able to pick up on lies from a client? How would you handle all the risk-taking behavior? Would you have gone to another state to get your child out of jail? Would you go after kids who got your child to use / distribute drugs?

6. Chapter 4: Rick's Teenage Years. Would you have gone on a wild goose chase after your son's girlfriend? Would you have helped your son out financially, so he wouldn't have to sell his plasma to pay his bills? Can you imagine having your grandkids in foster homes? What would you do if young kids were at your house and tried to hide food in their pockets to take home for later? Would you consider going to a worship service at a church very different from your own?

7. Chapter 6: My Own Personal Hell. Have you lived through times when you felt like you just didn't want to breathe anymore? Where the challenges you dealt with every day seemed insurmountable? Where the feelings of love for your spouse turned into more like the pain of an electrical shock? Could you go through a divorce?

8. Chapter 7: Rick's Growing Family. What would you do if narcotics were in the blood streams of your daughter and grand daughter at the time of birth? How would you feel if your grand kids were sent back to their parents who continued to use drugs? Could you accept a lawyer telling you you're not allowed to talk to your son? Would you be able to take in your brother's child because he and his wife couldn't provide for her as they continued to use drugs? Imagine what it was like to get shuffled around from house to house during your childhood and finally come to live with your grandpa, all the while wondering where you would go next. How would you feel if you could see your mom and dad only for a short visit once or twice a week? And during that time, you were under the watchful eye of a stranger from children's services, and you couldn't go home with them, or even play outside for a couple minutes. How would you feel toward the people who were now trying to take care of you in a foster home?

9. Chapter 8: New Living Situations. Would you be able to take in three grandchildren as a single grandparent while you were working in a job you loved? How would you handle telling your ten-year-old granddaughter that her mom died? Could you offer adequate grief support to your grandkids? Imagine losing your mom at age ten. Or five. Or three. Imagine finally concluding that you do not have the capacity to take care of someone who was born into your family and acknowledging that your grand daughter was born into your family to be raised in another family. Can you accept God's will to that extend? All the while not knowing where your son is? How do you think that loss would impact you over the years?

10. Chapter 9: Continuing Chaos. Would you read your child or grandchild's Facebook notifications if they came to your phone? Have your kids been caught shoplifting? Have they run away from home? How would you deal with uncontrollable, emotional flareups in your family?

11. Chapter 9: Getting Older, Finding Rick. A wise woman once said she thought it was harder having grandkids than kids because you have less control over how your grandkids are raised. Your thoughts? How would you feel if you didn't know if your son was dead or alive for six years? If you were an addict, and hadn't seen your children or been part of your family for six years, would you try to gat back in the fold? Can you imagine feeling apprehensive about spending time alone with your son? Would you consider holding your adult son tight through two slow dances? Or lying in bed with him, watching him breathe? Can you imagine hearing your son talk about his previous drug use? If you had custody of grandkids, would you be able to give them back to your son?

12. Chapter 11: Daisy Enters the Picture. Can you think of any issues that might come up related to Rick and Daisy getting engaged? How do you think Rick's kids felt about Rick spending so much time with Daisy and her kids?

13. Chapter 12: The Dominos Fall. Imagine your son (daughter, dad, mother) dying in an accident the day that was probably the happiest day of their life. Just imagine.

14. Chapter 13: Now Comes the Funeral. Would you be able to do the eulogy for your son? Would you have wanted your family closer to you during the funeral? Feel the emptiness in your heart when the hearse with your son's body pulled away from you for the last time.

15. Chapter 14: Gloom Despair and Agony on Me. How would you feel if your dead son's best friend texted you that you were a terrible, drunk mom? How would you feel if your grandkids got none of their inheritance from their dad? Have you ever felt entirely alone when you're in the depths of grief? What is an adequate length of time for a mother to grieve her son's death? Would you have had a service when you put your son's ashes with his wife's? What did you think of Hunter taking his dad's ashes to Daisy? What did you think of the house fire? Would you have gone to watch your childhood home burn down? What would you do at the holidays immediately following the death of your son? What would you do if your granddaughter was in the hospital, and the nurses were making fun of her? What do you think of Riley's description of drugs being something that you can't live without, yet know they will kill you?

16. Chapter 15 Our New Norm Can you feel my aloneness?

17. Katie Part 2: Safe Harbor. So now it's been seven years since I've seen my granddaughter. Would you be able to accept that? Would you try to forget about her? I continue to believe that she was born to my son to be raised by Chris and Melissa. How strong is your faith?

18. Afterthoughts. If it was you, would you be able to tell your story if you felt it was God's will?

Acknowledgments

I wish to thank so many of my family and friends who helped me get through some rough times just by being there to listen to my trials, comfort me in my losses, and encourage me to continue to live life fully when the going got tough. My sister, Florence Wenning has been my rock, a tower of strength for me. She has a way of getting me to talk about things that are hard for me to reckon with. My sister Jane, and her husband Nick Varney helped me come to grips with the craziness of my family. They always take my issues seriously, help me understand them, and eventually make me laugh about them. My friend, Ruth Anderson is such a kindred soul. She often provides me a reality check that I didn't know I needed. I have shared my deepest inner self with my best friend for life, Diane Hamilton (Heidi). She challenged me to do things I would have never considered when we were little girls. And she helped me grow through some very difficult times now that we're old grandmas.

I also wish to thank those who encouraged me to write this book. Kristy Matheson and Kelli Davis, who have told me since I met them many years ago that I should write books about my life and times. Jane and Nick Varney, as well as Ruth Anderson and Carol Scott-Maus have given me invaluable suggestions as the book developed. Kate Allison Hobbs and Jessica June Bair whom I work with, make me laugh—and just by that fact have helped me get through so much hell in the past year. They call me Aunt Nanc! I guess they like me, too! Another work mate, Mendy Simmons, keeps life real, and more bearable as we compare the menageries of our family relationships and interactions. It's nice to be around someone four days a week to talk about stuff that we each understand better about each other than almost anyone else could.

Although we don't always think in the same universe, I will always be grateful to Dale Wissman for stepping up to raise some grandkids when no one else could. The boys are developing into wonderful young men. And the girl is working through her early mistakes. I guess I don't need to agree with what he does for it to work for them. He's done such an awesome job. He truly is a hero not only to the kids, but to our entire family.

It goes without saying that my son "Josh" is often able to make me smile with his wit and help me to think deeply about our family situations. He continues to show me how heartaches can build up until reality is numbing. And then when the numbing subsides, the new reality often blossoms into a thing of joy.

I have always considered my daughter, Jennifer Creamer, to be wiser than I will ever be. I may not have always treated her like the princess she is, but I'm sure glad I didn't stop having kids after two! She is always the joy of my life.

Don and Judy Seger taught my son Rick so much about construction, roofing, and tree trimming. What he learned from them provided him with work for decades.

Two directors of the Social Work Department at Wright State University in Dayton Ohio, Dr. Carl Brun and Dr. Sarah Twill, have provided me with opportunities to pay forward to social work students. I met Carl when he awarded me the Wright State University Distinguished Social Worker College of Liberal Arts Alumna of the Year Award in 2011. Following that, he hired me to teach an Aging and End of Life class at Wright State University for three years. We also set up a Kids Night Out program at Wright State. This is a Friday evening of fun for foster kids in the area. Many of them are being raised by their grandparents. The kids get to be around young adults in the Social Work Club who are invigorating and intelligent—possibly the only young adults they have encountered who aren't stoned or abusive. And they get to play in the student union and even climb the rock wall. While they are having some fun, the foster parents get to have an evening to themselves. When they pick up the kids, the kids are exhausted from all the running around; they have temporary tattoos, they decorated cookies and crafts which they get to take home, and each of them has a smiling little red face from all the activity. Sarah has been able to keep the program alive and flourishing with the Alumni Social Work Club and sometimes other clubs getting involved. She also has been instrumental in helping me design a scholarship program for social work students at Wright State University. Pretty cool opportunities for a senior citizen, eh??

Scholarship

A portion of the proceeds from this book will benefit the Grieshop/ Wissman Endowed Social Work Scholarship Fund.

To contact the author for more information about the book or the scholarship, email Nancy at nancyshaus@live.com.

To give to the scholarship, contact:

The Wright State University Foundation
3640 Colonel Glenn Highway
Dayton, OH 45435-0001

Foundation Office: 937-775-4921

https://liberal-arts.wright.edu/connect/give-to-the-college

Thank you for your donation.

About the Author

Nancy Grieshop lives in southeastern Ohio. Her humble beginnings as the youngest in a large family didn't prepare her for the tumultuous life she would live as her son became a drug addict. She had no blueprint to follow as she muddled through one horrifying challenge after another. Yet she was able to draw on the strength of family, friends and her faith to get her through some impossibly difficult situations. Nancy writes with amazing clarity about her life circumstances. Her sense of humor flows through the trail of tears left in the wake of addiction. Her desire is to lend hope and strength to others who are dealing with addiction, have family members who are addicts, or those who work with addicts.

CPSIA information can be obtained
at www.ICGtesting.com
Printed in the USA
FFHW011326021118
49228439-53439FF

9 780982 218730